*Everyman, I will go with thee,
and be thy guide*

William Shakespeare

A MIDSUMMER NIGHT'S DREAM

Edited by
JOHN F. ANDREWS

Foreword by
F. MURRAY ABRAHAM

EVERYMAN
J.M. DENT · LONDON
CHARLES E. TUTTLE
VERMONT

Text © 1989 by Doubleday Book & Music Clubs, Inc

Textual revisions, revisions to notes, introduction, note on
text, chronology, and all end matter © J.M. Dent 1993

First published in Everyman by J.M. Dent 1993, Reprinted
1993, 1996
Published by permission of Guild America Books, an imprint
of Doubleday Book and Music Clubs, Inc.

Photoset by Deltatype Ltd, Ellesmere Port, Cheshire
Printed in Great Britain by
The Guernsey Press Co. Ltd., Guernsey, C.I.
for
J.M. Dent
Orion Publishing Group
Orion House
5 Upper St Martin's Lane, London WC2H 9EA
and
Charles E. Tuttle Co.
28 South Main Street, Rutland, Vermont
05701 5 USA

British Library Cataloguing-in-Publication-Data is available
upon request

ISBN 0 460 87246 X

CONTENTS

NOTE ON AUTHOR AND EDITOR

William Shakespeare is held to have been born on St George's day, 23 April 1564. The eldest son of a prosperous glove-maker in Stratford-upon-Avon, he was probably educated at the town's grammar school.

Tradition holds that between 1585 and 1592, Shakespeare first became a schoolteacher and then set off for London. By 1595 he was a leading member of the Lord Chamberlain's Men, helping to direct their business affairs, as well as being a playwright and actor. In 1598 he became a part-owner of the company, which was the most distinguished of its age. However, he maintained his contacts with Stratford, and his family seem to have remained there.

From about 1610 he seems to have grown increasingly involved in the towns affairs, suggesting a withdrawal from London. He died on 23 April 1616, in his 53rd year, and was buried at Holy Trinity Church on 25 April.

John F. Andrews has recently completed a 19-volume edition, *The Guild Shakespeare*, for the Doubleday Book and Music Clubs. He is also the editor of a 3-volume reference set, *William Shakespeare: His World, His Work, His Influence*, and the former editor (1974–85) of the journal *Shakespeare Quarterly*. From 1974–84, he was Director of Academic Programs at the Folger Shakespeare Library in Washington and Chairman of the Folger Institute.

CHRONOLOGY OF SHAKESPEARE'S LIFE

Year[1]	Age	Life
1564		Shakespeare baptised 26 April at Stratford-upon-Avon
1582	18	Marries Anne Hathaway
1583	19	Daughter, Susanna, born
1585	21	Twin son and daughter, Hamnet and Judith, born
1590–1	26	*The Two Gentlemen of Verona* & *The Taming of the Shrew*
1591	27	*2 & 3 Henry VI*
1592	28	*Titus Andronicus* & *1 Henry VI*
1592–3		*Richard III*
1593	29	*Venus and Adonis* published
1594	30	*The Comedy of Errors. The Rape of Lucrece* published
1594–5		*Love's Labour's Lost*
1595	31	*A Midsummer Night's Dream, Romeo and Juliet*, & *Richard II*. An established member of Lord Chamberlain's Men
1596	32	*King John*. Hamnet dies
1596–7		*The Merchant of Venice* & *1 Henry IV*
1597	33	Buys New Place in Stratford
		The Lord Chamberlain's Men's lease to play at the Theatre expires; until 1599 they play mainly at the Curtain

1 It is rarely possible to be certain about the dates at which plays of this period were written. For Shakespeare's plays, this chronology follows the dates preferred by Wells and Taylor, the editors of the Oxford Shakespeare. Publication dates are given for poetry and books.

CHRONOLOGY OF HIS TIMES

Year	Literary Context	Historical Events
1565–7	Golding, Ovid's *Metamorphoses*, tr.	Elizabeth I reigning
1574	*A Mirror for Magistrates* (3rd ed.)	
1576	London's first playhouse built	
1578	John Lyly, *Euphues*	
1579	North, Plutarch's *Lives*, tr.	
	Spenser, *Shepherd's Calender*	
1587	Marlowe, *I Tamburlaine*	Mary Queen of Scots
1588	Holinshed's *Chronicles* (2nd ed.)	executed
		Defeat of Spanish Armada
1589	Kyd, *Spanish Tragedy*	Civil war in France
	Marlowe, *Jew of Malta*	
1590	Spenser, *Faerie Queene*, Bks I–III	
1591	Sidney, *Astrophel and Stella*	Proclamation against Jesuits
1592	Marlowe, *Dr Faustus* & *Edward II*	Scottish witchcraft trials
		Plague closes theatres from June
1593	Marlowe killed	
1594	Nashe, *Unfortunate Traveller*	Theatres reopen in summer
1594–6		Extreme food shortages
1595	Sidney, *Defense of Poetry*	Riots in London
1596		Calais captured by Spanish
		Cadiz expedition
1597	Bacon's *Essays*	

Year	Age	Life
1597–8		*The Merry Wives of Windsor* & *2 Henry IV*
1598	34	*Much Ado About Nothing*
1598–9		*Henry V*
1599	35	*Julius Caesar*. One of syndicate responsible for building the Globe in Southwark, where the Lord Chamberlain's Men now play
1599–1600		*As You Like It*
1600–1		*Hamlet*
1601	37	*Twelfth Night*. His father is buried in Stratford
1602	38	*Troilus and Cressida*. Invests £320 in land near Stratford[2]
1603	39	*Measure for Measure*. The Lord Chamberlain's Men become the King's Men. They play at court more than all the other companies combined
1603–4		*Othello*
c.1604	40	Shakespeare sues Philip Rogers of Stratford for debt
1604–5		*All's Well That Ends Well*
1605	14	*Timon of Athens*. Invests £440 in Stratford tithes
1605–6		*King Lear*
1606	42	*Macbeth* & *Antony and Cleopatra*
1607	43	*Pericles*. Susanna marries the physician John Hall in Stratford
1608	44	*Coriolanus*. The King's Men lease Blackfriar's, an indoor theatre. His only grandchild is born. His mother dies
1609	45	*The Winter's Tale*. 'Sonnets' and 'A Lover's Complaint' published
1610	46	*Cymbeline*
1611	47	*The Tempest*
1613	49	*Henry VIII*. Buys houses in London for £140
1613–14		*The Two Noble Kinsmen*
1616	52	Judith marries Thomas Quiney, a vintner, in Stratford. On 23 April he dies, and is buried two days later
1623	59	Publication of the First Folio. His wife dies in August

2 A schoolmaster would earn around £20 a year at this time.

Year	Literary Context	Historical Events
1598	Marlowe and Chapman, *Hero and Leander* Jonson, *Every Man in his Humour*	Rebellion in Ireland
1599	Children's companies begin playing George Dekker's *Shoemaker's Holiday*	Essex fails in Ireland
1601	'War of the Theatres' Jonson, *Poetaster*	Essex rebels and is executed
1602		Tyrone defeated in Ireland
1603	Florio, Montaigne's *Essays*, tr.	Elizabeth I dies, James I accedes Raleigh found guilty of treason
1604	Marston, *The Malcontent*	Peace with Spain
1605	Bacon's *Advancement of Learning*	Gunpowder plot
1606	Jonson's *Volpone*	
1607	Tourneur, *The Revenger's Tragedy*, published	Virginia colonised Enclosure riots
1609		Oath of allegiance Truce in Netherlands
1610	Jonson, *Alchemist*	
1611	Authorised Version of the Bible Donne, *Anatomy of the World*	
1612	Webster, *White Devil*	Prince Henry dies
1613	Webster, *Duchess of Malfi*	Princess Elizabeth marries
1614	Jonson, *Bartholomew Fair*	
1616	Folio edition of Jonson's plays	

Biographical note, chronology and plot summary compiled by John Lee, University of Bristol, 1993.

by F. Murray Abraham

Shakespeare is boring. Let's be honest, isn't that what most people think? It's like going on a diet: you know it's good for you, but you can't wait till it's over – especially with his comedies.

With a tragedy, each member of the audience responds individually, privately, so that while *you* might be moved to tears, everyone around you might be asleep. This doesn't diminish your experience; it rather intensifies the sense of private communication with the actors, the play, and your own feelings. You have become a quiet participant in an evening that may change your life, even though everyone else is snoring – including the actors. I've given bad performances, yet afterwards some of these people would be waiting to thank me and to explain how much the performance meant to them. It is also true that after some of my most brilliant performances people have gone out of their way to avoid me. I believe their responses are sincere, but so are mine. There is simply no way to measure a tragedy during a performance other than privately.

Comedy, however, is public and requires a collective response. When you laugh out loud and everyone else is quiet, chances are you're not going to laugh again. With a tragedy you arrive in a serious frame of mind, and if you aren't carried away in the first act, you trust that by the second act something monumental is going to happen. Even if it doesn't, the material is usually rich enough to promise thoughtful rewards long after the night is over. Comedy can't wait. If you're not laughing in the first act you might not be there for the second. And you're right. If it's a comedy, it should be funny.

But how often have you gone to a Shakespeare comedy that is

so funny you can't wait to see it again? How often have you seen any comedy you really loved? For me, the dry spell between completely satisfying, lusty comedies lasted nearly fourteen years. So much time had passed that I began to doubt my memory, to wonder if perhaps I had imagined the one sweet show that reminded everyone why they loved the theatre. Oh, bits of it would surface from time to time, but never the unity of playwright, company, and audience that vibrates with pleasure. Never, that is, until *A Midsummer Night's Dream*.

Towards the end of this fabulous play Shakespeare gathers the entire company together with the audience to watch a tragedy performed by amateurs. The moment is designed to focus all attention on six comic characters, the mechanicals, who have been promising to be funny if they only had the chance. It's the moment every comic actor longs for and dreads, where the audience sits back, folds its arms and says, 'Show us your stuff,' and I know that the first actors who played these parts thought the same thing we did, 'If this doesn't work I'm going to wring Shakespeare's neck.'

There was no need to worry. People were rolling around in their seats; they were weeping and shouting with laughter. It's hard to believe a 400-year-old joke could go over so well. The backstage crew would sneak around to the front of the house and stand with the ushers to watch the finale every single time eight times a week. The cast of *Julius Caesar*, which was playing next door, in another auditorium of New York's Public Theatre, would show up in their togas to see as much as they could between entrances.

This gathering together of strangers so that they respond with one mind is nothing less than magic. At certain performances there were audiences spanning four generations, and the nine-year-olds were as delighted as their great-grandparents. They walked out of the theatre with grinning, surprised faces, and many came backstage to let us know they would return to see it again. Why did they insist on telling us? I suppose it was partly encouragement, but I think they also wanted to cling to that feeling we had all created together. We had discovered a great playwright who was as immediate and alive to us now as he was four centuries ago. And I promise you, not one of those audiences will ever again say that Shakespeare is boring.

F. MURRAY ABRAHAM's classical repertory extends from Sophocles to Shakespeare to Chekhov. His Shakespearean roles include Malvolio in *Twelfth Night*, the title role in *Macbeth*, Iago in *Othello*, and Bottom in *A Midsummer Night's Dream*. In 1984 he won an Academy Award for his portrayal of Salieri in the film *Amadeus*.

A Midsummer Night's Dream has long been one of Shakespeare's most popular works. It probes the very basis of artistic imagination, and it does so with a brilliance that has long made it a touchstone for writers, painters, composers, filmmakers, and philosophers with a compulsion to explore the mysteries of poetic vision. Its place in theatre history includes memorable productions by such influential directors as Samuel Phelps, Harley Granville-Barker, and Peter Brook. Its position in the musical repertory has been secure since the middle of the nineteenth century, when Felix Mendelssohn completed the orchestral score that remains his most popular composition. Its niche in the artist's studio has rewarded us with illustrations by painters of the stature of William Blake, Henry Fuseli, and George Cruikshank. And in our own century its role in the evolution of cinema has been scripted by filmmakers as distinctive as Max Reinhardt, Peter Hall, and Woody Allen.

Background

Just when Shakespeare wrote the play remains somewhat unclear, but most of the evidence points to the same period, 1594–96, when he was completing *Richard II* (whose lyricism has many stylistic similarities with *A Midsummer Night's Dream*) and *Romeo and Juliet* (which draws on some of the same source material in Ovid's *Metamorphoses*, and which seems in many ways to have been a tragic companion piece for the love trials treated comically in the world of Theseus' Athens.)

Many scholars believe that *A Midsummer Night's Dream* was either conceived or adapted for performance at a noble wedding attended in 1595 by Queen Elizabeth, to whom it pays an oblique compliment in II.i.155–64. If so, while presenting it Shakespeare and his colleagues would have found themselves in a position analogous to that of Peter Quince, Bottom, and the other 'rude Mechanicals' in their rendition of 'Pyramus and Thisby' before Theseus, the Duke of Athens, and his betrothed, Hippolyta. This would have made the play even more amusing than it is without such a context, and it would have added yet another level of irony and complexity to a work whose dislocations of perspective are already too confusing for anything but the most sophisticated dream analysis.

Comment on the Play

Within the play, of course, it is the wedding of Theseus and Hippolyta that frames the rest of the action. In the first scene Hermia is told that she has until the day of the Duke's solemn ceremony to decide whether she'll obey her father and marry Demetrius rather than Lysander. In the next scene the Athenian craftsmen who meet to rehearse their 'Interlude' do so because they hope to entertain the Duke and Duchess on the night of their nuptials. And in the third scene we learn that one of the reasons the King and Queen of the Fairies are now quarrelling in the Athenian woods is Oberon's affection for Hippolyta and his desire to be on hand to bless her marriage bed. As the play ends, Hermia's romantic difficulties are resolved, and she and the young man she loves are married along with Theseus and Hippolyta. The 'hempen Homespuns' are thrilled to receive word that their play is 'preferred'. And Oberon and Titania preside over a ritual in which Puck and the other Fairies consecrate the royal Palace and secure the newlyweds from harm.

But if concord prevails at the close of *A Midsummer Night's Dream*, it is achieved only at the price of a great medley of discord. In the opening scene, the Theseus whose sword has tamed the warring Amazons can resolve the dispute between Egeus and his daughter only by invoking a 'sharp Athenian Law' that forces Hermia and Lysander to flee in a desperate quest for freedom. Once they arrive in the woods, the lovers soon discover not only that they have been pursued there by Demetrius and Helena, but that all four youths are now at the mercy of an invisible Puck whose herbal ministrations, however well intended, turn friends into enemies and faithful lovers into infidels. Meanwhile the fairy quarrel that has disordered the seasons and turned all Nature topsy-turvy disrupts the Mechanicals' rehearsal: 'bully Bottom' the Weaver is 'translated' into an ass, and Oberon's lieutenant arranges for him to spend a night in the arms of a Titania who has been charmed into believing him the most beautiful creature she has ever seen. The result of all these mishaps is a lunatic tangle of misunderstandings in which we are shown that 'Reason and Love keep little Company nowadays'.

But of course that was something that had been clear from the opening scene in Athens. The miracle of Shakespeare's inspired plotting in *A Midsummer Night's Dream* is that he leads an astonishingly diverse collection of characters – and with them his audience – through an experience of frequently nightmarish madness to an eventual condition of sanity and harmony that can only be described, in Hippolyta's words, as 'strange and admirable'.

It is that capacity for the marvellous – that ability to take even so rock-bottom a sensibility as that of the imperturbable Weaver and transform it into something sublime – that Ralph Waldo Emerson was probably responding to when he referred to Shakespeare as 'inconceivably wise'. How the playwright achieved all his effects in *A Midsummer Night's Dream* is surely beyond our capacity to fathom. And that, no doubt, is one of the reasons we keep returning to the play, generation after generation, with such awe and joy.

John F. Andrews, 1993

THE TEXT OF THE EVERYMAN SHAKESPEARE

Background

THE EARLY PRINTINGS OF SHAKESPEARE'S WORKS

Many of us enjoy our first encounter with Shakespeare when we're introduced to *Julius Caesar* or *Macbeth* at school. It may therefore surprise us that neither of these tragedies could ever have been read, let alone studied, by most of the playwright's contemporaries. They began as scripts for performance and, along with seventeen other titles that never saw print during Shakespeare's lifetime, they made their inaugural appearance as 'literary' works seven years after his death, in the 1623 collection we know today as the First Folio.

The Folio contained thirty-six titles in all. Of these, half had been issued previously in the small paperbacks we now refer to as quartos.* Like several of the plays first published in the Folio, the most trustworthy of the quarto printings appear to have been set either from Shakespeare's own manuscripts or from faithful copies of them. It's not impossible that the poet himself prepared some of these works for the press, and it's intriguing to imagine him reviewing proof-pages as the words he'd written for actors to speak and embody were being transposed into the type that readers would filter through their eyes, minds, and imaginations. But, alas, there's no indisputable evidence that Shakespeare had any direct involvement with the publication of these early editions of his plays.

---

* Quartos derived their name from the four-leaf units of which these small books were comprised: large sheets of paper that had been folded twice after printing to yield four leaves, or eight pages. Folios, volumes with twice the page-size of quartos, were put together from two-leaf units: sheets that had been folded once after printing to yield four pages.

What about the scripts that achieved print for the first time in the Folio? Had the dramatist taken any steps to give the permanency of book form to those texts? We don't know. All we can say is that when he fell fatally ill in 1616, Shakespeare was denied any opportunities he might otherwise have taken to ensure that his 'insubstantial Pageants' survived the mortal who was now slipping into the 'dark Backward and Abysm of Time'.

Fortunately, two of the playwright's colleagues felt an obligation, as they put it, 'to procure his Orphans Guardians'. Sometime after his death John Heminge (or Heminges) and Henry Condell made arrangements to preserve Shakespeare's theatrical compositions in a manner that would keep them vibrant for the ages. They dedicated their endeavour to two noblemen who had helped see England's foremost acting company through some of its most trying vicissitudes. They solicited several poetic tributes for the volume, among them a now-famous eulogy by fellow writer Ben Jonson. They commissioned an engraved portrait of Shakespeare to adorn the frontispiece. And they did their utmost to display the author's dramatic works in a style that would both dignify them and make them accessible to 'the great Variety of Readers'.

As they prepared Shakespeare's plays for the compositors who would set them into stately Folio columns, Heminge and Condell (or editors designated to carry out their wishes) revised and augmented many of the entrances, exits, and other stage directions in the manuscripts. They divided most of the works into acts and scenes.* For a number of plays they appended 'Names of the Actors', or casts of characters. Meanwhile they made every effort to guarantee that the Folio printers had reliable copy-texts for each of the titles: authoritative manuscripts for the plays that had not been published previously, and good quarto printings (annotated in some instances to insert staging details, mark script changes, and add supplementary material) for the ones that had been issued prior to the Folio. For several titles they supplied texts

* The early quartos, reflecting the unbroken sequence that probably typified Elizabethan and Jacobean performances of the plays, had been printed without the structural demarcations usual in Renaissance editions of classical drama.

that were substantially different from, if not always demonstrably superior to, the quarto versions that preceded them.

Like even the most accurate of the printings that preceded it, the Folio collection was flawed by minor blemishes. But it more than fulfilled the purpose of its generous-minded compilers: 'to keep the memory of so worthy a Friend and Fellow alive as was our Shakespeare'. In the process it provided a publishing model that remains instructive today.

MODERN EDITIONS OF THE PLAYS AND POEMS

When we compare the First Folio and its predecessors with the usual modern edition of Shakespeare's works, we're more apt to be impressed by the differences than by the similarities. Today's texts of Renaissance drama are normally produced in conformity with twentieth-century standards of punctuation and usage; as a consequence they look more neat, clean, and, to our eyes, 'right' than do the original printings. Thanks to an editorial tradition that extends back to the early eighteenth century and beyond, most of the rough spots in the early printings of Shakespeare have long been smoothed away. Textual scholars have ferreted out redundancies and eradicated inconsistencies. They've mended what they've perceived to be errors and oversights in the playscripts, and they've systematically attended to what they've construed as misreadings by the copyists and compositors who transmitted those playscripts to posterity. They've added '[Within]' brackets and other theatrical notations. They've revised stage directions they've judged incomplete or inadequate in the initial printings. They've regularized disparities in the speech headings. They've gone back to the playwright's sources and reinstated the proper forms for many of the character and place names which a presumably hasty or inattentive author got 'wrong' as he conferred identities on his dramatis personae and stage locales. They've replaced obsolete words like *bankrout* with their modern heirs (in this case *bankrupt*). And in a multitude of other ways they've accommodated Shakespeare to the tastes, interests, and expectations of latter-day readers.

The results, on the whole, have been splendid. But interpreting the artistic designs of a complex writer is always problematical, and the task is especially challenging when that writer happens to have been a poet who felt unconstrained by many of the 'rules' that more conventional dramatists respected. The undertaking becomes further complicated when new rules, and new criteria of linguistic and social correctness, are imposed by subsequent generations of artists and critics.

To some degree in his own era, but even more in the neoclassical period (1660–1800) that came in its wake, Shakespeare's most ardent admirers thought it necessary to apologise for what Ben Jonson hinted at in his allusion to the 'small Latin, and less Greek' of an untutored prodigy. To be sure, the 'sweet Swan of Avon' sustained his popularity; in fact his reputation rose so steadily that by the end of the eighteenth century he'd eclipsed Jonson and his other peers and become the object of near-universal Bardolatry. But in the theatre most of his plays were being adapted in ways that were deemed advisable to tame their supposed wildness and bring them into conformity with the decorum of a society that took pride in its refinement. As one might expect, some of the attitudes that induced theatre proprietors to metamorphose an unpolished poet from the provinces into something closer to an urbane man of letters also influenced Shakespeare's editors. Persuaded that the dramatist's works were marred by crudities that needed expunging, they applied their ministrations to the canon with painstaking diligence.

Twentieth-century editors have moved away from many of the presuppositions that guided a succession of earlier improvers. But a glance at the textual apparatus accompanying virtually any modern publication of the plays and poems will show that emendations and editorial procedures deriving from such forebears as the sets published by Nicholas Rowe (1709), Alexander Pope (1723–25, 1728), Lewis Theobald (1733, 1740, 1757), Thomas Hanmer (1743–45, 1770–71), Samuel Johnson (1765), Edward Capell (1768), George Steevens (1773), and Edmond Malone (1790) retain a strong hold on today's renderings of the playwright's works. The consequence is a 'Shakespeare' who offers the tidiness we've come to expect in our libraries of treasured authors, but not necessarily the playwright a 1599 reader of the Second Quarto of *Romeo and Juliet* would still be able to recognize as a contemporary.

OLD LIGHT ON THE TOPIC

Over the last two decades we've learned from art curators that paintings by Old Masters such as Michelangelo and Rembrandt look a lot brighter when centuries of grime are removed from their surfaces – when hues that had become dulled with soot and other extraneous matter are allowed to radiate again with something approximating their pristine luminosity. We've learned from conductors like Christopher Hogwood that there are aesthetic rewards to be gained from a return to the scorings and instruments with which Renaissance and Baroque musical compositions were first presented. We've learned from twentieth-century experiments in the performance of Shakespeare's plays that an open, multi-level stage, analogous to that on which the scripts were originally enacted, does more justice to their dramaturgical techniques than does a proscenium auditorium devised for works that came later in the development of Western theatre. We've learned from archaeological excavations in London's Bankside area that the foundations of playhouses such as the Rose and the Globe look rather different from what many historians had expected. And we're now learning from a close scrutiny of Shakespeare's texts that they too look different, and function differently, when we accept them for what they are and resist the impulse to 'normalize' features that strike us initially as quirky, unkempt, or unsophisticated.

The Aims that Guide the Everyman Text

Like other modern editions of the dramatist's plays and poems, The Everyman Shakespeare owes an incalculable debt to the scholarship that has led to so many excellent renderings of the author's works. But in an attempt to draw fresh inspiration from the spirit that animated those remarkable achievements at the outset, the Everyman edition departs in a number of respects from the usual post-Folio approach to the presentation of Shakespeare's texts.

RESTORING SOME OF THE NUANCES OF
RENAISSANCE PUNCTUATION

In its punctuation, Everyman attempts to give equal emphasis to sound and sense. In places where Renaissance practice calls for heavier punctuation than we'd normally employ – to mark the caesural pause in the middle of a line of verse, for instance – Everyman sometimes retains commas that other modern editions omit. Meanwhile, in places where current practice usually calls for the inclusion of commas – after vocative and interjections such as 'O' and 'alas', say, or before 'Madam' or 'Sir' in phrases such as 'Ay Madam' or 'Yes Sir' – Everyman follows the original printings and omits them.

Occasionally the absence of a comma has a significant bearing on what an expression means, or can mean. At one point in *Othello*, for example, Iago tells the Moor 'Marry patience' (IV.i.90). Inserting a comma after 'Marry', as most of today's editions do, limits Iago's utterance to one that says 'Come now, have patience.' Leaving the clause as it stands in the Folio, the way the Everyman text does, permits Iago's words to have the additional, agonizingly ironic sense 'Be wed to Patience'.

The early texts generally deploy exclamation points quite sparingly, and the Everyman text follows suit. Everyman also follows the early editions, more often than not, when they use question marks in places that seem unusual by current standards: at the ends of what we'd normally treat as exclamations, for example, or at the ends of interrogative clauses in sentences that we'd ordinarily denote as questions in their entirety.

The early texts make no orthographic distinction between simple plurals and either singular or plural possessives, and there are times when the context doesn't indicate whether a word spelled *Sisters*, say, should be rendered *Sisters*, *Sisters'*, or *Sister's* in today's usage. In such situations the Everyman edition prints the word in the form modern usage prescribes for plurals.

REVIVING SOME OF THE FLEXIBILITY OF
RENAISSANCE SPELLING

Spelling had not become standardized by Shakespeare's time, and that meant that many words could take a variety of forms. Like James Joyce and some of the other innovative prose and verse stylists of our own century, Shakespeare revelled in the freedom a largely unanchored language provided, and with that in mind Everyman retains original spelling forms (or adaptations of those forms that preserve their key distinctions from modern spellings) whenever there is any reason to suspect that they might have a bearing on how a word was intended to be pronounced or on what it meant, or could have meant, in the playwright's day. When there is any likelihood that multiple forms of the same word could be significant, moreover, the Everyman text mirrors the diversity to be found in the original printings.

In many cases this practice affects the personalities of Shakespeare's characters. One of the heroine's most familiar questions in *Romeo and Juliet* is 'What's in a Name?' For two and a half centuries readers – and as a consequence actors, directors, theatre audiences, and commentators – have been led to believe that Juliet was addressing this query to a Romeo named 'Montague'. In fact 'Montague' *was* the name Shakespeare found in his principal source for the play. For reasons that will become apparent to anyone who examines the tragedy in detail, however, the playwright changes his protagonist's surname to 'Mountague', a word that plays on both 'mount' and 'ague' (fever). Setting aside an editorial practice that began with Lewis Theobald in the middle of the eighteenth century, Everyman resurrects the name the dramatist himself gave Juliet's lover.

Readers of *The Merchant of Venice* in the Everyman set will be amused to learn that the character modern editions usually identify as 'Lancelot' is in reality 'Launcelet', a name that calls attention to the clown's lusty 'little lance'. Like Costard in *Love's Labour's Lost*, another stage bumpkin who was probably played by the actor Will Kemp, Launcelet is an upright 'Member of the Commonwealth'; we eventually learn that he's left a pliant wench 'with Child'.

Readers of *Hamlet* will find that 'Fortinbras' (as the name of the Prince's Norwegian opposite is rendered in the First Folio and in most modern editions) appears in the earlier, authoritative 1604 Second Quarto of the play as 'Fortinbrasse'. In the opening scene of that text a surname that meant 'strong in arms' in French is introduced to the accompaniment of puns on *brazen*, in the phrase 'brazon Cannon', and on *metal*, in the phrase 'unimprooued mettle'. In the same play readers of the Everyman text will encounter 'Ostricke', the ostrich-like courtier who invites the Prince of Denmark to participate in the fateful fencing match that draws *Hamlet* to a close. Only in its final entrance direction for the obsequious fop does the Second Quarto call this character 'Osric', the name he bears in all the Folio text's references to him and in most modern editions of Shakespeare's most popular tragedy.

Readers of the Everyman *Macbeth* will discover that the fabled 'Weird Sisters' appear only as the 'weyward' or 'weyard' Sisters. Shakespeare and his contemporaries knew that in his *Chronicles of England, Scotland, and Ireland* Raphael Holinshed had used the term 'weird sisters' to describe the witches who accost Macbeth and Banquo on the heath; but no doubt because he wished to play on *wayward*, the playwright changed their name to *weyward*. Like Samuel Johnson, who thought punning vulgar and lamented Shakespeare's proclivity to seduction by this 'fatal Cleopatra', Lewis Theobald saw no reason to retain the playwright's weyward spelling of the witches' name. He thus restored the 'correct' form from Holinshed, and editors ever since have generally done likewise.

In many instances Renaissance English had a single spelling for what we now define as two separate words. For example, *humane* combined the senses of 'human' and 'humane' in modern English. In the First Folio printing of *Macbeth* the protagonist's wife expresses a concern that her husband is 'too full o'th' Milke of humane kindnesse'. As she phrases it, *humane kindnesse* can mean several things, among them 'humankind-ness', 'human kindness', and 'humane kindness'. It is thus a reminder that to be true to his or her own 'kind' a human being must be 'kind' in the sense we now attach to 'humane'. To disregard this logic, as the protagonist and his wife will soon prove, is to disregard a principle as basic to the cosmos as the laws of gravity.

In a way that parallels *humane*, *bad* could mean either 'bad' or 'bade', *borne* either 'born' or 'borne', *ere* either 'ere' (before) or 'e'er' (ever), *least* either 'least' or 'lest', *lye* either 'lie' or 'lye', *nere* either 'ne'er' or 'near' (though the usual spellings for the latter were *neare* or *neere*), *powre* either 'pour' or 'power', *then* either 'than' or 'then', and *tide* either 'tide' or 'tied'.

There are a number of word-forms that functioned in Renaissance English as interchangeable doublets. *Travail* could mean 'travel', for example, and *travel* could mean 'travail'. By the same token, *deer* could mean *dear* and vice versa, *dew* could mean *due*, *hart* could mean *heart*, and (as we've already noted) *mettle* could mean *metal*.

A particularly interesting instance of the equivocal or double meanings some word-forms had in Shakespeare's time is *loose*, which can often become either 'loose' or 'lose' when we render it in modern English. In *The Comedy of Errors* when Antipholus of Syracuse compares himself to 'a Drop / Of Water that in the Ocean seeks another Drop' and then says he will 'loose' himself in quest of his long-lost twin, he means both (a) that he will release himself into a vast unknown, and (b) that he will lose his own identity, if necessary, to be reunited with the brother for whom he searches. On the other hand, in *Hamlet* when Polonius says he'll 'loose' his daughter to the Prince, he little suspects that by so doing he will also lose his daughter.

In some cases the playwright employs word-forms that can be translated into words we wouldn't think of as related today: *sowre*, for instance, which can mean 'sour', 'sower', or 'sore', depending on the context. In other cases he uses forms that do have modern counterparts, but not counterparts with the same potential for multiple connotation. For example, *onely* usually means 'only' in the modern sense; but occasionally Shakespeare gives it a figurative, adverbial twist that would require a nonce word such as 'one-ly' to replicate in current English.

In a few cases Shakespeare employs word-forms that have only seeming equivalents in modern usage. For example, *abhominable*, which meant 'inhuman' (derived, however incorrectly, from *ab*, 'away from', and *homine*, 'man') to the poet and his contemporaries, is not the same word as our *abominable* (ill-omened, abhorrent). In his advice to the visiting players Hamlet complains about incompetent actors who imitate 'Humanity so abhominably' as to make the characters they depict seem unrecognizable as men. Modern readers who don't realize the distinction between Shakespeare's word and our own, and who see *abominable* on the page before them, don't register the full import of the Prince's satire.

Modern English treats as single words a number of word-forms that were normally spelled as two words in Shakespeare's time. What we render as *myself*, for example, and use primarily as a reflexive or intensifying pronoun, is almost invariably spelled *my self* in Shakespeare's works; so also with *her self*, *thy self*, *your self*, and *it self* (where *it* functions as *its* does today). Often there is no discernible difference between Shakespeare's usage and our own. At other times there is, however, as we are reminded when we come across a phrase such as 'our innocent self' in *Macbeth* and think how strained it would sound in modern parlance, or as we observe when we note how naturally the same is objectified in the balanced clauses of the Balcony Scene in *Romeo and Juliet*:

> Romeo, doffe thy name,
> And for thy name, which is no part of thee,
> Take all my selfe.

Yet another difference between Renaissance orthography and our own can be exemplified with words such as *today*, *tonight*, and *tomorrow*, which (unlike *yesterday*) were treated as two words in Shakespeare's time. In *Macbeth* when the Folio prints 'Duncan comes here to Night', the unattached *to* can function either as a preposition (with *Night* as its object, or in this case its destination) or as the first part of an infinitive (with *Night* operating figuratively as a verb). Consider the ambiguity a Renaissance reader would have detected in the original publication of one of the most celebrated soliloquies in all of Shakespeare:

> To morrow, and to morrow, and to morrow,
> Creeps in this petty pace from day to day,
> To the last Syllable of Recorded time:
> And all our yesterdayes, have lighted Fooles
> The way to dusty death.

Here, by implication, the route 'to morrow' is identical with 'the way to dusty death', a relationship we miss if we don't know that for Macbeth, and for the audiences who first heard these lines spoken, *to morrow* was not a single word but a potentially equivocal two-word phrase.

RECAPTURING THE ABILITY TO HEAR WITH OUR EYES
When we fail to recall that Shakespeare's scripts were designed initially to provide words for people to hear in the theatre, we sometimes overlook a fact that is fundamental to the artistic structure of a work like *Macbeth*: that the messages a sequence of sounds convey through the ear are, if anything, even more significant than the messages a sequence of letters, punctuation marks, and white spaces on a printed page transmit through the eye. A telling illustration of this point, and of the potential for ambiguous or multiple implication in any Shakespearean script, may be found in the dethronement scene of *Richard II*. When Henry Bullingbrook asks the King if he is ready to resign his crown, Richard replies 'I, no no I; for I must nothing be.' Here the punctuation in the 1608 Fourth Quarto (the earliest text to print this richly complex passage) permits each *I* to signify either 'ay' or 'I' (*I* being the usual spelling for 'ay' in Shakespeare's time).

Understanding *I* to mean 'I' permits additional play on *no*, which can be heard (at least in its first occurrence) as 'know'. Meanwhile the second and third soundings of *I*, if not the first, can also be heard as 'eye'. In the context in which this line occurs, that sense echoes a thematically pertinent passage from Matthew 18:9: 'if thine eye offend thee, pluck it out'.

But these are not all the implications *I* can have here. It can also represent the Roman numeral for '1', which will soon be reduced, as Richard notes, to 'nothing' (o), along with the speaker's title, his worldly possessions, his manhood, and eventually his life. In Shakespeare's time, to become 'nothing' was, *inter alia*, to be emasculated, to be made a 'weaker vessel' (1 Peter 3:7) with 'no thing'. As the Fool in *King Lear* reminds another monarch who has abdicated his throne, a man in want of an 'I' is impotent, 'an O without a Figure' (I.iv.207). In addition to its other dimensions, then, Richard's reply is a statement that can be formulated mathematically, and in symbols that anticipate the binary system behind today's computer technology: '1, o, o, 1, for 1 must o be.'

Modern editions usually render Richard's line 'Ay, no; no, ay; for I must nothing be'. Presenting the line in that fashion makes good sense of what Richard is saying. But as we've seen, it doesn't make total sense of it, and it doesn't call attention to Richard's paradoxes in the same way that hearing or seeing three undifferentiated *I*'s is likely to have done for Shakespeare's contemporaries. Their culture was more attuned than ours is to the oral and aural dimensions of language, and if we want to appreciate the special qualities of their dramatic art we need to train ourselves to 'hear' the word-forms we see on the page. We must learn to recognize that for many of what we tend to think of as fixed linkages between sound and meaning (the vowel 'I', say, and the word 'eye'), there were alternative linkages (such as the vowel 'I' and the words 'I' and 'Ay') that could be just as pertinent to what the playwright was communicating through the ears of his theatre patrons at a given moment. As the word *audience* itself may help us to remember, people in Shakespeare's time normally spoke of 'hearing' rather than 'seeing' a play.

In its text of *Richard II*, the Everyman edition reproduces the title character's line as it appears in the early printings of the tragedy. Ideally the orthographic oddity of the repeated *I*'s will encourage today's readers to ponder Richard's utterance, and the play it epitomizes, as a characteristically Shakespearean enigma.

OTHER ASPECTS OF THE EVERYMAN TEXT

Now for a few words about other features of the Everyman text.

One of the first things readers will notice about this edition is its bountiful use of capitalized words. In this practice as in others, the Everyman exemplar is the First Folio, and especially the works in the Folio sections billed as 'Histories' and 'Tragedies'.* Everyman makes no attempt to adhere to the Folio printings with literal exactitude. In some instances the Folio capitalizes words that the Everyman text of the same passage lowercases; in other instances Everyman capitalizes words not uppercased in the Folio. The objective is merely to suggest something of the flavour, and what appears to have been the rationale, of Renaissance capitalization, in the hope that today's audiences will be made continually aware that the works they're contemplating derive from an earlier epoch.

Readers will also notice that instead of cluttering the text with stage directions such as '[Aside]' or '[To Rosse]', the Everyman text employs unobtrusive dashes to indicate shifts in mode of address. In an effort to keep the page relatively clear of words not supplied by the original printings, Everyman also exercises restraint in its addition of editor-generated stage directions. Where the dialogue makes it obvious that a significant action occurs, the Everyman text inserts a square-bracketed phrase such as '[Fleance escapes]'. Where what the dialogue implies is subject

---

* The quarto printings employ far fewer capital letters than does the Folio. Capitalization seems to have been regarded as a means of recognizing the status ascribed to certain words (*Noble*, for example, is almost always capitalized), titles (not only King, Queen, Duke, and Duchess, but Sir and Madam), genres (tragedies were regarded as more 'serious' than comedies in more than one sense), and forms of publication (quartos, being associated with ephemera such as 'plays', were not thought to be as 'grave' as the folios that bestowed immortality on 'works', writings that, in the words of Ben Jonson's eulogy to Shakespeare, were 'not of an age, but for all time').

to differing interpretations, however, the Everyman text provides a facing-page note to discuss the most plausible inferences.

Like other modern editions, the Everyman text combines into 'shared' verse lines (lines divided among two or more speakers) many of the part-lines to be found in the early publications of the plays. One exception to the usual modern procedure is that Everyman indents some lines that are not components of shared verses. At times, for example, the opening line of a scene stops short of the metrical norm, a pentameter (five-foot) or hexameter (six-foot) line comprised predominantly of iambic units (unstressed syllables followed by stressed ones). In such cases Everyman uses indentation as a reminder that scenes can begin as well as end in mid-line (an extension of the ancient convention that an epic commences *in medias res*, 'in the midst of the action'). Everyman also uses indentation to reflect what appear to be pauses in the dialogue, either to allow other activity to transpire (as happens in *Macbeth*, II.iii.87, when a brief line 'What's the Business?' follows a Folio stage direction that reads '*Bell rings. Enter Lady.*') or to permit a character to hesitate for a moment of reflection (as happens a few seconds later in the same scene when Macduff responds to a demand to 'Speak, speak' with the reply 'O gentle Lady, / 'Tis not for you to hear what I can speak').

Everyman preserves many of the anomalies in the early texts. Among other things, this practice pertains to the way characters are depicted. In *A Midsummer Night's Dream*, for example, the ruler of Athens is usually identified in speech headings and stage directions as 'Theseus', but sometimes he is referred to by his title as 'Duke'. In the same play Oberon's merry sprite goes by two different names: 'Puck' and 'Robin Goodfellow'.

Readers of the Everyman edition will sometimes discover that characters they've known, or known about, for years don't appear in the original printings. When they open the pages of the Everyman *Macbeth*, for example, they'll learn that Shakespeare's audiences were unaware of any woman with the title 'Lady Macbeth'. In the only authoritative text we have of the Scottish tragedy, the protagonist's spouse goes by such names as 'Macbeth's Lady', 'Macbeth's Wife', or simply 'Lady', but at no time is she listed or mentioned as 'Lady Macbeth'. The same is true of the character usually designated 'Lady Capulet' in modern editions of *Romeo and Juliet*. 'Capulet's Wife' makes appearances as 'Mother', 'Old Lady', 'Lady', or simply 'Wife'; but she's never termed 'Lady Capulet', and her husband never treats her with the dignity such a title would connote.

Rather than 'correct' the grammar in Shakespeare's works to eliminate what modern usage would categorize as solecisms (as when Mercutio says 'my Wits faints' in *Romeo and Juliet*), the Everyman text leaves it intact. Among other things, this principle applies to instances in which archaic forms preserve idioms that differ slightly from related modern expressions (as in the clause 'you are too blame', where 'too' frequently functions as an adverb and 'blame' is used, not as a verb, but as an adjective roughly equivalent to 'blameworthy').

Finally, and most importantly, the Everyman edition leaves unchanged any reading in the original text that is not manifestly erroneous. Unlike other modern renderings of Shakespeare's works, Everyman substitutes emendations only when obvious problems can be dealt with by obvious solutions.

The Everyman *Text of* A Midsummer Night's Dream

The primary authority for modern editions of *A Midsummer Night's Dream* is the 1600 First Quarto (Q1), which many scholars believe to have been set directly from a copy of the playwright's own script. A Second Quarto (Q2), falsely dated 1600, appeared in 1619. It introduced a few alterations in the text and added a handful of minor stage directions. There is no reason to ascribe any textual weight to it, however, because it was almost certainly an unauthorized reprint of the First Quarto.

The Folio text (F1) appears to have been set from an annotated copy of the Second Quarto. It provides act divisions (but not scene divisions, which must therefore be inserted by modern editors), and it supplies a number of stage directions not to be found in the

First Quarto. Its main differences from the First Quarto text occur in Act V, where (a) Egeus replaces Philostrate as Master of the Revels, (b) a few speech headings are assigned to characters other than those designated to speak the same lines in Q1, and (c) a handful of what may have been authorial revisions are substituted for Q1 readings.

The Everyman edition follows the First Quarto more closely than do most modern editions. Among other things, the Everyman text retains far more of the First Quarto's commas than do most of today's printings of the play. Everyman also differs from other twentieth-century editions of *A Midsummer Night's Dream* in its treatment of Act V, which has two scenes rather than the one conventionally marked in modern renderings of the play.

Like other editions, Everyman incorporates most of the stage directions added by the Folio printers. These include entrances (at III.i.102, III.ii.438, V.i.170, 317), exits (at II.i.244, II.ii.93, III.i.106, III.ii.101, IV.i.189, 202, 224, IV.ii.46, V.i.208), one music cue (at IV.i.86), and several indications of stage action (such as 'Shifting places' at III.ii.416, 'Bottom wakes' at IV.i.202, and inaction (such as the references to lying down or sleeping at II.ii.71, III.ii.418, 436).

Everyman also adopts Folio alterations of Q1 spelling variants in a number of passages where retaining the Quarto word-form would misrepresent what the context indicates to be the intended meaning. Thus the reader will find *off* rather than *of* in II.i.183, III.ii.260, and IV.i.68, *prey* rather than *pray* in II.ii.156, and *too* rather than *to* in III.ii.313. Similarly, Everyman follows the Folio in altering *their* to *there* in I.i.74, *hear* to *here* in I.i.133, *the* to *thee* in II.i.194, *Minnick* to *Mimic* in III.ii.19, *slippe* to *sleep* in III.ii.85, *or* to *o'er* in IV.i.76, *howe* to *ho* in IV.i.86, and *or* to *our* in V.i.34.

In a number of passages Everyman adopts what appear to be either (a) Q2 or F1 corrections of Q1 errors, or (b) authorial revisions incorporated into the Folio text. Thus Everyman alters the text from *waues* to *wanes* in I.i.4, from *West* to *the West* in

II.i.158, from *not* to *nor* in II.i.201, from *comfor* to *Comfort* in II.ii.44, from *Bet it* to *Be it* in II.ii.45, from *it* to *is* in II.ii.53, from *Cet.* to *Bottom* in the speech heading for III.i.56, from *Quince* to *Puck* in the speech heading for III.i.88, from *Gentleman* to *Gentlemen* in III.ii.299, from *shat* to *shalt* in III.ii.426, from *this* to *this is* in IV.i.131, from *expound* to *to expound* in IV.i.210, from *Flute* to *Starveling* in the speech heading for IV.ii.3, from *lets* to *let us* in IV.i.202, from *Flute* to *Snout* in V.i.158, from *mow again* to *knit up in thee* in V.i.194, and from *Moon used to Moral down* in V.i.209. Everyman also prints (though without confidently endorsing) the Folio's addition of *passionate* in II.ii.20.

In two instances Everyman adopts corrections introduced by Nicholas Rowe in his 1700 edition of the play, changing from *Your* to *To your* in III.ii.451, and from *Lions* to *Lion* in V.ii.1. Everyman also follows other modern editions in the speech headings it inserts in II.ii.13, 24 and in III.i.164–69. In one instance where the evidence is ambiguous in the early printings, Everyman does what most modern editions do and assigns III.i.51 to Snout rather than Snug. In both Q1 and F1 this speech heading is abbreviated *Sn.*, so either character could be given the line; the 1632 Second Folio assigned it to Snug. In another instance, V.ii.49–50, where two lines appear in both Q1 and F1 in what is evidently the incorrect sequence, Everyman follows the practice of other modern editions and transposes them.

Far more often than it accords with the emendations adopted by other modern editions, however, the Everyman text adheres to the readings in the First Quarto. Most of these instances are discussed in the facing-page notes, but it might be valuable to enumerate the most significant divergences between the Everyman text and most twentieth-century editions of *A Midsummer Night's Dream*. For each passage in the following list the first entry, set in boldface type, is the Everyman reading; the second is the emendation usually adopted by today's editors of the play.

I.i.   10 **Now bent** New-bent
       19 S.D. **and Helena** *omitted*
       23 S.D. **Stand forth Demetrius** *set as dialogue*

25 S.D. **Stand forth Lysander** *set as dialogue*
31 **faining . . . faining** *either* faining . . . feigning *or* feigning
. . . feigning
72 **barrain** barren (so also in III.ii.13)
114 **loose** lose (so also in II.i.206, III.ii.252, V.i.306)
136 **Love** low
154 **dew** due
187 **your Words** yours would
191 **I'll** I'd
216 **swell'd** sweet
219 **strange Companions** stranger companies

I.ii.   11 **Mary** Marry (so also in V.i.362)
28 **rest** rest –
31 **split** split.
41 **Vain** vein

II.i.   61 **Fairy** Fairies
69 **Steppe** steep *or* step
78 **Perigenia** Perigouna
79 **him, with fair Eagles,** him with fair Aegles
Faith faith,
101 **humane** human (so also in II.ii.125)
here cheer
109 **Chin** thin
151 **hermonious** harmonious
162 **chast** chaste
181 **medling** meddling
190 **stay . . . stayeth** slay . . . slayeth
192 **wodde** wood
238 **I** Ay (so also in III.ii.277)

II.ii.   49 **god** good
71 **prest** press'd
129 **borne** born (so also in III.ii.124)

III.i.   2 **marvailes** marvellous (so also in IV.i.26)
29–30 **your self** yourselves
32 **wild Foul** wild-fowl (compare III.ii.20)
70 **Or let** and let
84 **Odours, 'odorous'** odors, odors
200 **you** you of

III.ii.	6	**in love,** in love.
	7	**Bower.** bower,
	80	**part I** part I so
	137	**perfect Divine** perfect, divine (compare line 227)
	142	**Fand** fann'd
	164	**hear** here (compare I.i.133)
	170	**ere** e'er
	175	**Least** lest (so also in III.ii.385)
	213	**first Life-coats** first, like coats
	237	**I do** Ay, do!
	250	**Praise** prayers
	279	**of Doubt** doubt
	406	**Speak in some Bush.** Speak! In some bush?
IV.i.	21	**curtsy** courtesy
	44	**always** all ways
	85	**Sleep: of all these, fine the Sense** Sleep of all these five the sense
	120	**Seem** Seem'd
	136	**Right** rite
	175	**see** saw
	213	**patch'd a Fool** a patch'd fool
	219	**Ballet** ballad
IV.ii.	26	**Harts** hearts
	30	**not true** no true
V.i.	124	**Recorder, a Sound;** recorder; a sound,
	143	**scarre** scare
	220	**Beasts, in a** beasts in, a
	276	**Beams** gleams
	321	**Moth** mote
	323	**warnd** warrant
	331	**dumbe** dumb
	332	**Tumbe** tomb
	348	**imbrew** imbrue
	355	**S.H. Lion** Bottom
	372	**Gate** gait (so also in V.ii.46)
V.ii.	2	**beholds** behowls
	4	**foredoone** fordone
	22	**Fier** fire

Finally, the Everyman text of *A Midsummer Night's Dream* retains a number of spelling forms that indicate subtle differences between Shakespeare's English and our own. Among those forms are the following: *auncient, Boord, chaung'd, chaunting, Cuckow, daunce, deflour'd, despight, Devise* (for device), *Dewlop, divelish, Divels, every where, Flouriets, foorth, glaunce, graunt, Hoord, Maisters, Marchandise, me thinks, mounch, perchaunce, perfit, Phantasy, queint, Rimes, rosted, Sheepherd's, shew'd, shrike, Spight, to morrow,* and *Woosel.*

A MIDSUMMER NIGHT'S DREAM

NAMES OF THE ACTORS

THESEUS, Duke of Athens
HIPPOLYTA, Queen of the Amazons, betrothed to Theseus
PHILOSTRATE, Theseus' Master of the Revels

EGEUS, Father to Hermia
HERMIA, Maiden, in love with Lysander
HELENA, Hermia's friend, in love with Demetrius
LYSANDER, Suitor to Hermia, beloved by her
DEMETRIUS, Suitor to Hermia, endorsed by her Father

OBERON, King of the Fairies
TITANIA, Queen of the Fairies
PUCK, or ROBIN GOODFELLOW, Sprite in Oberon's service

A FAIRY
PEASEBLOSSOM
COBWEB } Fairies in Titania's service
MOTH
MUSTARDSEED

PETER QUINCE, a Carpenter; Prologue in the Interlude
NICK BOTTOM, a Weaver; Pyramus in the Interlude
FRANCIS FLUTE, a Bellows-Mender; Thisby in the Interlude
TOM SNOUT, a Tinker; Wall in the Interlude
SNUG, a Joiner; Lion in the Interlude
ROBIN STARVELING, a Tailor; Moonshine in the Interlude

LORDS AND ATTENDANTS to Theseus and Hippolyta

4

I.i.   The setting for the opening scene is the palace of Theseus, a
        legendary Athenian hero who has just defeated the Amazons,
        a tribe of warlike women. He is now preparing to wed their
        Queen, Hippolyta, whom he has captured in battle (line 16).

1   **our Nuptial Hour**   the hour of our wedding.

2   **apace**   at a brisk pace.

2-3   **four . . . An other Moon**   Although it is often thought that this
        play is bathed in moonlight, the action actually takes place
        during the darkest phase of the lunar cycle, with only a
        glimmering of light on the scene. It is, significantly, a time of
        change, a point Hippolyta will reiterate in V.i.253-54.

4-6   **she . . . Revenue**   Theseus compares his impatience ('she lingers
        my desires') to that of a young man whose inheritance is
        wasting away in the hands of a stepmother or dowager (a
        widow who holds title to, or continues drawing income from,
        an estate) for as long as she 'withers'. Here *wanes* is adopted
        from the First Folio printing (1623). The 1600 First Quarto
        prints *waues* (waves).

7   **steep . . . Night**   This phrase evokes an image of the Sun
        dropping below the horizon to soak in an ocean of darkness.

10   **Now bent**   These words appear in both the First Quarto and
        First Folio printings of the play. Most editors emend them to
        'New-bent'; but since the original reading makes good sense,
        there is no need to alter it. In this speech Hippolyta is telling
        her fiancé to be patient. Four days, she says, will pass as
        quickly as if they had been dreamt away. Besides, the Moon is
        already 'bent' like a 'Bow' on the verge of dispatching the
        arrow that will signify nuptial consummation. As it happens,
        the 'Four Days' turn out to be two days and one night of
        dramatized action.

11   **Solemnities**   dignified but joyous ceremonies; the 'Pomp' (line
        15) that befits a royal wedding.

13   **pert and nimble**   lively and youthful; the opposite of
        'withering'.
        Spirit   here pronounced in a gliding fashion, so as to constitute
        a single syllable metrically. Cheered by Hippolyta's comment,
        Theseus seeks to banish all despondency, including his own.

15   **Pale Companion**   Melancholy is called a 'Pale Companion'
        because of its association with the sequestered life of
        contemplation.

ACT I

Scene 1

Enter Theseus, Hippolyta, [Philostrate,] with Others.

THESEUS   Now, fair Hippolyta, our Nuptial Hour
Draws on apace: four happy Days bring in
An other Moon. But O, me thinks, how slow
This Old Moon wanes: she lingers my Desires
Like to a Stepdame or a Dowager,   5
Long withering out a Young Man's Revenue.
HIPPOLYTA   Four Days will quickly steep themselves
    in Night;
Four Nights will quickly dream away the Time;
And then the Moon, like to a silver Bow,
Now bent in Heaven, shall behold the Night   10
Of our Solemnities.
THESEUS   Go, Philostrate,
Stir up the Athenian Youth to Merriments.
Awake the pert and nimble Spirit of Mirth;
Turn Melancholy forth to Funerals:
The Pale Companion is not for our Pomp.   15
                                        [*Exit Philostrate.*]
– Hippolyta, I woo'd thee with my Sword,
And won thy Love, doing thee Injuries.

6

19   **With Pomp, with Triumph**   In contrast to Melancholy, the pale companion (line 15), 'Pomp' (spectacle) and public 'Triumph' (celebration) will attend the forthcoming marriage of Theseus and Hippolyta.

19
S.D.   The Quarto lists Helena among the characters who enter here. Most editors omit her, but it is not inconceivable that she is a silent observer of the exchanges that follow.

23
S.D.   **Stand forth Demetrius**   Like the stage direction that follows it, this is usually interpreted as a command delivered by Egeus. Both imperatives would complete the half-lines that follow, and it may thus be correct to infer that the Quarto and Folio printers misinterpreted the script they were typesetting. But both imperatives would also serve quite satisfactorily as directives to the actors playing Demetrius and Lysander, perhaps with Egeus silently but firmly indicating when they should 'Stand forth'.

31   **faining Voice . . . faining Love**   Although both words are spelled 'faining' in the First Quarto and First Folio texts, we now have different words to discriminate between 'longing' or 'singing softly' (faining) and 'faking' (feigning).

32   **Phantasy**   fantasy; imagination, fancy. This spelling reflects the Greek origin of the word (compare *phantasm* and *phantom*).

33   **Gauds, Conceits**   fancy 'Knacks' (knick-knacks) and intricate 'Trifles'.

35   **unhardened Youth**   Egeus assumes that Hermia is so unformed ('unhardened') in character and thus so impressionable ('as a form of Wax', line 49), that her affections can be fashioned by the trinkets ('Gauds'), elegant fineries ('Conceits'), and other childish favours (lines 33–34) given to her by Lysander. In *Othello*, I.iii, Brabantio accuses the title character of using even more sinister means to bewitch a maiden daughter to fall in love with him.

37   **due to me**   both (a) entirely of my making (since I 'imprinted' the form she bears), and (b) owed to me as the holder of her bond of indebtedness.

39   **Be it so**   if it happens that.

But I will wed thee in another Key:
With Pomp, with Triumph, and with Revelling.

Enter Egeus and his daughter Hermia, and Lysander and
Helena and Demetrius.

EGEUS   Happy be Theseus, our renowned Duke.   20
THESEUS   Thanks, good Egeus. What's the News with
    thee?
EGEUS   Full of Vexation come I, with Complaint
Against my Child, my daughter Hermia.

Stand forth Demetrius.

My Noble Lord,
This Man hath my consent to marry her.   25

Stand forth Lysander.

And my gracious Duke,
This Man hath bewitch'd the Bosom of my Child.
– Thou, thou, Lysander, thou hast given her
    Rimes
And interchang'd Love-tokens with my Child;
Thou hast, by Moonlight, at her Window sung,   30
With faining Voice, Verses of faining Love,
And stol'n th' Impression of her Phantasy
With Bracelets of thy Hair, Rings, Gauds,
    Conceits,
Knacks, Trifles, Nosegays, Sweetmeats (Messengers
Of strong Prevailment in unhardened Youth);   35
With Cunning hast thou filch'd my Daughter's
    Heart,
Turn'd her Obedience, which is due to me,
To stubborn Harshness. – And, my gracious Duke,
Be it so she will not here, before your Grace,

41 **auncient Privilege of Athens** prerogative allowed to fathers by time-honoured Athenian law and custom.

47 **To you ... God** Theseus tells Hermia that as her begetter, her father has absolute authority over her. Thus her duty is to submit the impressions of her 'Eyes' to his 'Judgement' (line 57).

51 **disfigure** literally, 'unmake', mar. The verb reappears in III.i.61.

54 **in this kind** in this case.
wanting your Father's Voice lacking your father's consent.

59 **Power** Owing to its metrical position in the line, *power* is here pronounced as a gliding one-syllable word. In line 50, on the other hand, its position at the conclusion of the verse line (where an additional unstressed syllable was permitted at the end of the final foot for a 'feminine ending') allows it to be treated, depending on the speaker's wish, as either a one-syllable or a two-syllable word.

60 **Nor how it may concern my Modesty** nor whether it is in keeping with the behaviour fitting a virtuous maiden.

61 **In such a Presence** in such a solemn setting as your Grace's court.

65 **to die the Death** to be executed.

68 **your Blood** your feelings and 'Desires' (line 67, echoing line 4); the promptings of the passionate part of your nature. But *Blood* can also mean inherited nobility, as in line 135.

70 **the Livery of a Nun** Theseus depicts the nun's 'Livery' ('habit' in two senses) as if it, too, meant a kind of death: 'faint', 'cold', 'fruitless', and 'barrain' (barren, but here spelled in a way that plays on *brain* to emphasize the aridity of pale contemplation).

71 **For aye** forever. Compare line 90.
mew'd (a) encaged, cooped up, like a hawk that is 'mewing' (moulting, a sense reinforced by *barrain* in line 72), and (b) uttering the faint mewing sounds of a cat or seagull (compare line 73).

Consent to marry with Demetrius,   40
I beg the auncient Privilege of Athens:
As she is mine, I may dispose of her,
Which shall be either to this Gentleman
Or to her Death, according to our Law
Immediately provided in that case.   45

THESEUS   What say you, Hermia? Be advis'd, fair
   Maid,
  To you your Father should be as a God;
  One that compos'd your Beauties, yea, and one
  To whom you are but as a Form in Wax,
  By him imprinted, and within his Power   50
  To leave the Figure or disfigure it.
  Demetrius is a worthy Gentleman.

HERMIA   So is Lysander.

THESEUS   In himself he is;
  But in this kind, wanting your Father's Voice,
  The other must be held the worthier.   55

HERMIA   I would my Father look'd but with my Eyes.

THESEUS   Rather your Eyes must with his Judgement
  look.

HERMIA   I do entreat your Grace to pardon me:
  I know not by what Power I am made bold,
  Nor how it may concern my Modesty,   60
  In such a Presence, here to plead my Thoughts;
  But I beseech your Grace that I may know
  The worst that may befall me in this case
  If I refuse to wed Demetrius.

THESEUS   Either to die the Death or to abjure   65
  For ever the Society of Men.
  Therefore, fair Hermia, question your Desires,
  Know of your Youth, examine well your Blood,
  Whether, if you yield not to your Father's
    Choice,
  You can endure the Livery of a Nun,   70
  For aye to be in shady Cloister mew'd,

76–78 **earthlier happy is the Rose Distill'd . . . Blessedness** The rose
that is plucked so that its essence can be preserved in perfume
is of more earthly value than that which wilts without
perpetuating itself. *Withering* recalls line 6. Compare Sonnet
5.

80   **Virgin Patent** virginity.

81   **unwished Yoke** undesired 'Lordship' (rule over me as his wife).

84   **Sealing Day** day to put an official wax seal ('Impression', line
32) on our 'Bond of Fellowship' (line 85). Theseus portrays
marriage as a contract between equals who devoutly wish to
be yoked together.

89   **Diana's Altar to protest** Diana, Goddess of the Moon, was also
the Goddess of Chastity; her votaries were required to profess
('protest') a life of austere privation.

92   **crazed Title** untenable and thus insane claim. *Crazed* literally
meant 'cracked', as in the glaze on a piece of pottery.

97   **Right of her** rights in her. Both here and in line 92, *Right* can
also mean 'rite'; compare IV.i.136.

98   **estate unto** bestow upon, give title to.

99   **well deriv'd** well born. Lysander goes on to say that he is as
well possessed of wealth and standing ('Fortunes') as
Demetrius. Lysander may be appealing to Theseus to overrule
Egeus (and perhaps even speaking privately to the Duke), but
he may also be making one last attempt to persuade Egeus to
change his mind.

101–2 **as . . . vantage** esteemed as highly, if not more highly. *Fortunes*
could be construed to mean *Fortune's*.

105   **prosecute my Right** pursue my own claims.

106   **avouch it to his Head** maintain it ('my Right') to his face.

To live a barrain Sister all your Life,
Chaunting faint Hymns to the cold fruitless Moon.
Thrice blessed they that master so their Blood
To undergo such maiden Pilgrimage;   75
But earthlier happy is the Rose Distill'd
Than that which, withering on the Virgin Thorn,
Grows, lives, and dies in Single Blessedness.

HERMIA   So will I grow, so live, so die, my Lord,
Ere I will yield my Virgin Patent up   80
Unto his Lordship whose unwished Yoke
My Soul consents not to give Sovereignty.

THESEUS   Take time to pause, and by the next New
    Moon,
The Sealing Day betwixt my Love and me,
For everlasting Bond of Fellowship,   85
Upon that Day either prepare to die
For Disobedience to your Father's Will,
Or else to wed Demetrius as he would,
Or on Diana's Altar to protest
For aye Austerity and Single Life.   90

DEMETRIUS   Relent, sweet Hermia; and Lysander, yield
Thy crazed Title to my certain Right.

LYSANDER   You have her Father's Love, Demetrius;
Let me have Hermia's; do you marry him.

EGEUS   Scornful Lysander, true, he hath my Love;   95
And what is mine my Love shall render him.
And she is mine, and all my Right of her
I do estate unto Demetrius.

LYSANDER   I am, my Lord, as well deriv'd as he,
As well possess'd; my Love is more than his;   100
My Fortunes every way as fairly rank'd,
If not with vantage, as Demetrius';
And, which is more than all these Boasts can be,
I am belov'd of beauteous Hermia.
Why should not I then prosecute my Right?   105
Demetrius, I'll avouch it to his Head,

107   **Made love to**   The modern meaning of the phrase is inapplicable here. Lysander is saying that Demetrius wooed Helena with what Egeus would call 'faining Love' (line 31), exchanged betrothal vows with her ('won her Soul', line 108), and then forsook her to pursue Hermia.

110   **Spotted and Inconstant**   tainted and unreliable.

113   **self affairs**   my own concerns.

114   **loose**   both (a) release, and (b) lose track of.

116   **Schooling**   counsel, instruction.

117   **your self**   Normally spelled as two words in the Elizabethan period (as is *my self*), when *self* was treated somewhat more objectively than the modern spelling of *myself* and *yourself* encourages.

118   **fit your Fancies to your Father's Will**   The alliterative *f*'s in this line aptly focus the contending forces in the opening scene.

120   **extenuate**   weaken, mitigate; literally, 'thin out'.

121   **Single Life**   unmarried life, celibacy. Compare line 90.

123   **go along**   come along with me. Here, and frequently elsewhere in Shakespeare's plays, *go* means 'walk'. Compare *Romeo and Juliet*, I.i.103–6, where another quarrel ends with the ruler arranging private conferences designed to restore harmony to his city.

125   **Against our Nuptial**   in preparation for our wedding.

126   **nearly ... selves**   that touches you closely.

130–   **Belike ... Eyes**   Hermia means: Perhaps for lack of rain, which
31   I could well supply them with from my tearful eyes.

136   **O ... Love**   Both the First Quarto and First Folio texts read *love*. 'Low', an emendation adopted by most editors, supplies a neat contrast with 'High'. But Hermia may mean only that her own high station makes it impossible for her to be 'enthrall'd' to 'Love', rather than to her 'Father's Will' (line 118) and thus to 'Blood' regarded as equal in rank.

137   **Misgraffed**   misgrafted, mismatched. All the 'crosses' listed in lines 135–41 result from various kinds of 'misgrafting': in 'Blood' (birth of station), in 'Years', and in the liberty to choose with one's own eyes.

Made love to Nedar's daughter Helena
And won her Soul; and she, sweet Lady, dotes,
Devoutly dotes, dotes in Idolatry,
Upon this Spotted and Inconstant Man.   110
THESEUS   I must confess that I have heard so much,
And with Demetrius thought to have spoke thereof;
But being over full of self affairs,
My Mind did loose it. – But Demetrius, come,
And come, Egeus, you shall go with me: 115
I have some private Schooling for you both.
– For you, fair Hermia, look you arm your self
To fit your Fancies to your Father's Will;
Or else the Law of Athens yields you up
(Which by no means we may extenuate)   120
To Death or to a Vow of Single Life.
– Come, my Hippolyta: what cheer, my Love?
– Demetrius and Egeus, go along:
I must employ you in some business
Against our Nuptial, and confer with you   125
Of something nearly that concerns your selves.
EGEUS   With Duty and Desire we follow you.
                    Exeunt [all but Lysander and Hermia].
LYSANDER   How now, my Love? Why is your Cheek so
   pale?
How chance the Roses there do fade so fast?
HERMIA   Belike for want of Rain, which I could well   130
Beteem them from the Tempest of my Eyes.
LYSANDER   Ay me! for aught that I could ever read,
Could ever hear by Tale or History,
The Course of True Love never did run smooth.
But either it was different in Blood –   135
HERMIA   O Cross! too High to be enthrall'd to Love.
LYSANDER   Or else Misgraffed in respect of Years –
HERMIA   O Spight! too Old to be engag'd to Young!
LYSANDER   Or else it stood upon the Choice of
   Friends –

143 **momentany** [from Latin *momentaneus*] momentary.

145– **Brief . . . Confusion** This passage depicts lightning as a brilliant
49   'bright thing' that discloses ('unfolds') both earth and sky
before being instantly chewed to bits (brought to 'Confusion')
in the 'Jaws of Darkness'. *Collied* means coal-black, but may
also suggest 'choleric' by its association with 'in a Spleen' (fit
of rage), a phrase deriving from the view that the spleen was
the seat of impulsive anger. *Quick* can function either as an
adjective (meaning both 'living' and 'speedy') or as an adverb
(meaning 'quickly').

151 **Edict** The metre dictates that this word be accented on the
second syllable. The same is true of *Revenue* in line 158. In
line 6 above, on the other hand, the metre calls for our usual
pronunciation of *Revenue*, stressing the first syllable.

154 **As dew to Love** as much an aspect of love. *Dew* (echoing line
37) means *due*; but its spelling reinforces 'Tears' (line 155).

155 **Fancy's Followers** Love's disciples. *Fancy* (from *fantasy*) is a
complex term that relates to all those emotional and
imaginative powers habitually contrasted with reason. It often
means love or desire, as in this instance.

159 **remote** removed, distant. Lines 157–60 echo lines 3–6. The
'Dowager' Lysander refers to would 'linger' (prolong) his
'Desires' in a way he would welcome, not lament like
Theseus.
   seven Leagues twenty-one miles. A league is three miles.

160 **respects** both (a) loves, and (b) thinks of, regards.

162 **sharp** severe, harsh.

165 **without** outside.

170 **golden Head** an allusion to Book I of Ovid's narrative poem
Metamorphoses, where Cupid employs a golden-headed
arrow to ignite love and a leaden-headed arrow to extinguish
it.

171 **Venus' Doves** Doves were sacred to Venus, the Goddess of
Love. Their 'simplicity' (innocence and fidelity) was
proverbial.

172 **knitteth** joins, interweaves.

HERMIA   O Hell, to choose Love by another's Eyes!   140
LYSANDER   Or if there were a Sympathy in
   Choice,
  War, Death, or Sickness did lay siege to it,
  Making it momentany as a Sound,
  Swift as a Shadow, short as any Dream,
  Brief as the Lightning in the collied Night,   145
  That in a Spleen unfolds both Heaven and Earth,
  And ere a Man hath power to say 'Behold,'
  The Jaws of Darkness do devour it up:
  So quick bright things come to Confusion.
HERMIA   If then True Lovers have been ever cross'd,   150
  It stands as an Edict in Destiny.
  Then let us teach our trial Patience:
  Because it is a customary Cross,
  As dew to Love as Thoughts, and Dreams, and Sighs,
  Wishes and Tears, poor Fancy's Followers.   155
LYSANDER   A good Persuasion. Therefore hear me,
   Hermia:
  I have a widow Aunt, a Dowager,
  Of great Revenue, and she hath no Child;
  From Athens is her House remote seven Leagues,
  And she respects me as her only Son.   160
  There, gentle Hermia, may I marry thee;
  And to that place the sharp Athenian Law
  Cannot pursue us. If thou lovest me then,
  Steal forth thy Father's House to morrow Night,
  And in the Wood, a League without the Town   165
  (Where I did meet thee once with Helena
  To do observance to a Morn of May),
  There will I stay for thee.
HERMIA   My good Lysander,
  I swear to thee by Cupid's strongest Bow,
  By his best Arrow, with the golden Head,   170
  By the simplicity of Venus' Doves,
  By that which knitteth Souls and prospers Loves,

173 **Carthage Queen** Dido. In Book IV of Virgil's *Aeneid*, when Dido realizes that Aeneas, 'the false Troyan' (line 174), has left her, she commits suicide on a funeral pyre.

180 **Whither away?** Where are you going? Evidently Helena, upon seeing Hermia, seeks to avoid an encounter with her. Hermia's phrasing echoes lines 6 and 77, and thereby reminds us that Hermia and Lysander are trying to avoid withering away as victims of Athenian tyranny.

182 **your Fair** your kind of light complexion; as we shall see, Hermia's complexion is darker than Helena's.

183 **Loadstars** guiding stars, lodestars with the magnetic pull of loadstones (lodestones).
Air melody.

184 **tuneable** melodious.

186 **catching** contagious. Helena then goes on to play on other meanings of *catch*: (a) to hear, register (line 187), (b) to capture and make mine (line 188), and (c) to sing a 'catch' or round of music (line 189).
Favour both (a) beauty, and (b) the love beauty attracts.

187 **Your . . . catch** I register what you say when you call me 'fair Helena' [but what I really need is the 'Favour' that would make me 'Fair' indeed]. Most editors emend *Your Words* to *Yours would*; no alteration is needed.

190 **bated** excepted. Helena is willing to give up all the world, with the exception of one person (Demetrius), in order to change identities with Hermia ('be to you translated', line 191). *Bated* can also mean 'excited, but held in check' (as in *Romeo and Juliet*, III.ii.14), and that sense would also fit Helena's wishes.

191 **translated** transformed or transported. This word anticipates III.i.119–20 and IV.ii.3–4.

195– **O . . . mine** The rapid-fire exchanges here (illustrating a device
201 known as 'stichomythia', first used in Greek tragedy) depend upon the balanced antitheses in phrases such as 'The more I hate . . .' and 'The more I love . . .' The comparisons and contrasts in these lines are reinforced by the rhyming couplets into which the exchanges are organized.

And by that Fire which burn'd the Carthage Queen
When the false Troyan under sail was seen,
By all the Vows that ever Men have broke   175
(In Number more than ever Women spoke),
In that same place thou hast appointed me
To morrow truly will I meet with thee.
LYSANDER   Keep promise, Love. Look, here comes
     Helena.

Enter Helena.

HERMIA   God speed, fair Helena! Whither away?   180
HELENA   Call you me Fair? That Fair again unsay.
   Demetrius loves your Fair: O happy Fair!
   Your Eyes are Loadstars, and your Tongue's sweet
       Air
   More tuneable than Lark to Shepherd's Ear
   When Wheat is green, when Hawthorn Buds appear.   185
   Sickness is catching; O, were Favour so.
   Your Words I catch, fair Hermia; ere I go
   My Ear should catch your Voice, my Eye your Eye;
   My Tongue should catch your Tongue's sweet
       Melody.
   Were the World mine, Demetrius being bated,   190
   The rest I'll give to be to you translated.
   O teach me how you look, and with what Art
   You sway the Motion of Demetrius' Heart.
HERMIA   I frown upon him, yet he loves me still.
HELENA   O that your Frowns would teach my Smiles
     such Skill.   195
HERMIA   I give him Curses, yet he gives me Love.
HELENA   O that my Prayers could such Affection move.
HERMIA   The more I hate, the more he follows me.
HELENA   The more I love, the more he hateth me.
HERMIA   His Folly, Helena, is no Fault of mine.   200

208 **unfold** open up, disclose.

209 **Phoebe** another name for Diana, Goddess of the Moon, and hence of the Moon itself. *Behold* echoes lines 9–11.

210 **wat'ry Glass** mirroring water.

212 **still** ever, always.

213 **devis'd** arranged, planned.

215 **wont** accustomed. *Faint* recalls line 73.

216 **Counsel swell'd** The First Quarto and First Folio read *counsel swell'd*, which, despite the break in the pattern of rhyming couplets, makes good sense and seems likely to reflect Shakespeare's intent. Most editors emend *swell* to *sweet* to yield a rhyme with *meet* in line 217. Hermia's phrasing looks forward to II.i.123–37.

219 **strange Companions** new acquaintances, companions who are now but strangers to us. Although these words appear in the First Quarto and First Folio, most editors emend them to *stranger companies* in order to continue the sequence of rhyming couplets. *Companions* recalls line 15. Little does Hermia realize what 'strange Companions' she and Lysander will find in the woods.

226 **othersome** some others.

230– **And ... Qualities** Helena is saying that just as Demetrius errs
31   in thinking Hermia fairer than she, so Helena errs in her infatuation with '*his* Qualities'.

232 **Quantity** substance, something that can be measured. Compare III.ii.131–33.

233 **transpose** translate. Compare lines 190–91.

HELENA   None but your Beauty; would that Fault were
   mine.
HERMIA   Take Comfort: he no more shall see my Face;
   Lysander and my self will fly this Place.
   Before the time I did Lysander see
   Seem'd Athens as a Paradise to me;   205
   O then what Graces in my Love do dwell
   That he hath turn'd a Heaven unto a Hell!
LYSANDER   Helen, to you our Minds we will unfold:
   To morrow Night, when Phoebe doth behold
   Her silver Visage in the wat'ry Glass,   210
   Decking with liquid Pearl the bladed Grass
   (A time that Lovers' Flights doth still conceal),
   Through Athens' Gates have we devis'd to steal.
HERMIA   And in the Woods where often you and I
   Upon faint Primrose Beds were wont to lie,   215
   Emptying our Bosoms of their Counsel swell'd,
   There my Lysander and my self shall meet,
   And thence from Athens turn away our Eyes
   To seek new Friends and strange Companions.
   Farewell, sweet Playfellow; pray thou for us,   220
   And good Luck graunt thee thy Demetrius.
   – Keep word, Lysander; we must starve our Sight
   From Lovers' Food till morrow deep Midnight.
LYSANDER   I will, my Hermia.   *Exit Hermia.*
                 – Helena, adieu:
   As you on him, Demetrius dote on you.   225
                        Exit Lysander.
HELENA   How happy some o'er othersome can be!
   Through Athens I am thought as fair as she.
   But what of that? Demetrius thinks not so:
   He will not know what all but he do know.
   And as he errs, doting on Hermia's Eyes,   230
   So I, admiring of his Qualities.
   Things Base and Vile, holding no Quantity,
   Love can transpose to Form and Dignity.

235 **painted Blind** Normally the eye was considered the organ most subject to deception. Helena associates childish fancy with the mind instead, using the word to refer not to the reason but to such faculties as memory, imagination, and will.

237 **Wings . . . Haste** Helena pictures Cupid, the God of Love, as having 'Wings and no Eyes'. In her 'figure' (emblematic picture), Cupid is characterized by rashness ('unheedy Haste') rather than sound judgement. Helena may not realize that there was another well-known interpretation of the emblem of blind Cupid that saw him as a symbol of the higher Platonic love that judges not by the eyes (subject to deception and susceptible to passion) but by the reason.

239 **beguil'd** deceived, cheated. Compare II.i.45.

240 **forswear** break their oaths, perjure themselves.

242 **Eyne** archaic for 'eyes'. This line would seem to contradict Helena's generalization about love looking only 'with the Mind' (line 234).

249 **dear Expense** not 'a large expense' (the usual meaning of this phrase), but an expense that may endear her to Demetrius. But Helena may also mean that if all her 'Pain' (trouble) yields her is 'Thanks' it *will* be a 'dear Expense', one that costs much pain (suffering).

I.ii This scene takes place somewhere in Athens. The craftsmen we meet here are reminiscent of the guild artisans who produced dramatic pageants ('interludes') in Tudor England. The names of the rustics (later referred to as 'Clowns' or bumpkins) reflect their work: 'Quince' probably comes from the 'quoins' or wedges used by carpenters; 'Snug' is a fit name for a cabinet-maker; 'Bottom' is a name for the core or spool on which a weaver's yarn was wound; 'Flute' suggests the thin-voiced man who mends wind instruments such as flute organs and bellows; 'Snout' evokes the nozzle or spout familiar to one who mends pots and kettles; and 'Starveling' derives from the proverbial image of the emaciated tailor.

2 **generally** as a group. What Bottom means is 'severally' or 'individually'. Like most of the labouring classes depicted in Shakespeare, the tradesmen here speak either in prose or in doggerel verse.

3 **Scrip** script. *Scrip* could also refer to a small bag or wallet, or to a scrap of paper, a 'scroll' (line 16).

Love looks not with the Eyes, but with the Mind:
And therefore is wing'd Cupid painted Blind.   235
Nor hath Love's Mind of any Judgement taste:
Wings and no Eyes figure unheedy Haste.
And therefore is Love said to be a Child:
Because in Choice he is so oft beguil'd.
As waggish Boys in game themselves forswear,   240
So the boy Love is perjur'd every where.
For ere Demetrius look'd on Hermia's Eyne,
He hail'd down Oaths that he was only mine;
And when this Hail some Heat from Hermia felt,
So he dissolved, and Show'rs of Oaths did melt.   245
I will go tell him of fair Hermia's Flight:
Then to the Wood will he to morrow Night
Pursue her; and for this Intelligence
If I have Thanks, it is a dear Expense.
But herein mean I to enrich my Pain,   250
To have his Sight thither and back again.

Exit.

Scene 2

*Enter Quince the Carpenter, and Snug the Joiner, and Bottom
the Weaver, and Flute the Bellows-Mender, and Snout the
Tinker, and Starveling the Tailor.*

QUINCE   Is all our Company here?
BOTTOM   You were best to call them generally, Man
by Man, according to the Scrip.
QUINCE   Here is the Scroll of every man's Name, which
is thought fit, through all Athens, to play in   5
our Interlude, before the Duke and the Duchess,
on his Wedding Day at Night.
BOTTOM   First, good Peter Quince, say what the Play

10   **grow to a Point**   come to a conclusion. Bottom's phrasing hints
      inadvertently at male tumescence (compare *Hamlet*,
      I.v.124–29), and it anticipates such passages as IV.ii.7–8 and
      V.i.362–65. Compare II.ii.121–28 and V.i.118–20.

11   **Mary**   a mild oath (usually spelled *marry* by Shakespeare's
      time) that originally referred to the Virgin Mary.

11–13 **our . . . Thisby**   In the title for the 'Pyramus and Thisbe'
      playlet, as well as in the crudity of its poetry and dramatic
      effects, Shakespeare is poking fun at such works as a 1570
      play advertised as 'A lamentable tragedy mixed ful of pleasant
      mirth, conteyning the life of Cambyses, King of Percia'.

16–17 **spread your selves**   Bottom probably means 'disperse yourselves
      so that we'll have room to rehearse without restraint'.

20   **Part**   dramatic character. But 'Part' often alludes to bodily parts
      (including those that 'grow to a Point' and expire 'most
      gallant, for Love'). Bottom's own name suggests one part of
      the human anatomy, as does 'Tailor'.

25   **ask**   call for.

28   **condole**   express grief.
      to the rest yet   either (a) as for my other dramatic talents, or (b)
      turning to the other parts to be assigned. Most editors move
      the Quarto's comma so that it precedes *yet* rather than
      following it.

29   **Humour**   temperamental disposition.

30   **Ercles**   Hercules.

31   **split**   Most editors insert a stop after *split*. But it seems perfectly
      in character for Bottom to 'make all split the raging Rocks'.
      Like Peter Quince, he's not one to 'stand upon Points'
      (V.i.118).

41   **Ercles' Vain**   Hercules' vein or manner. The Quarto spelling of
      Vain is an amusing reminder of how 'lofty' (vainglorious)
      Bottom's Ercles is. Bottom's pronunciation of names such as
      Hercules and Phoebus ('Phibbus', line 36) is in keeping with
      his generally unsophisticated approach to drama and
      literature.

treats on; then read the Names of the Actors;
and so grow to a Point.   10

QUINCE   Mary, our Play is 'The most lamentable
Comedy and most cruel Death of Pyramus and
Thisby'.

BOTTOM   A very good Piece of Work, I assure you,
and a merry. Now, good Peter Quince, call forth   15
your Actors by the Scroll. – Masters, spread
your selves.

QUINCE   Answer as I call you. – Nick Bottom the
Weaver?

BOTTOM   Ready. Name what Part I am for, and
proceed.   20

QUINCE   You, Nick Bottom, are set down for Pyramus.

BOTTOM   What is Pyramus? A Lover, or a Tyrant?

QUINCE   A Lover that kills himself, most gallant,
for Love.

BOTTOM   That will ask some Tears in the true   25
Performing of it. If I do it, let the Audience
look to their Eyes. I will move Storms; I will
condole, in some measure. To the rest yet, my
chief Humour is for a Tyrant. I could play
Ercles rarely, or a Part to tear a Cat in, to   30
make all split
      The raging Rocks
      And shivering Shocks
      Shall break the Locks
         Of prison Gates.   35
      And Phibbus' Car
      Shall shine from far
      And make and mar
         The foolish Fates.
This was lofty. Now, name the rest of the   40
Players. This is Ercles' Vain, a Tyrant's
Vain; a Lover is more condoling.

QUINCE   Francis Flute, the Bellows-Mender?

46 **wand'ring Knight**   knight-errant. In this scene Shakespeare
catalogues and burlesques the character types who dominated
a more primitive stage of Elizabethan drama. In this edition
Thisby, Shakespeare's rustic spelling for the *Thisbe* of Ovid's
Metamorphoses, is retained in the text along with *Phibbus*,
Ercles, and other homespun forms.

50 **all one**   all the same; of no moment.
Mask   the protective shield women wore outdoors to protect
their fair complexions.

51 **small**   befitting a young or feminine speaker.

53 **monstrous**   'terribly' (line 75); extraordinarily.

54 **Thisne**   Here Bottom adopts a 'monstrous little Voice' for a
high-pitched, 'small' rendering of the heroine's name.

66 **fitted**   equipped with parts.

68 **slow of study**   not adept at learning a part.

69 **extempore**   extemporaneously, ad-libbing. The Quarto comma
before *extempore*, retained here along with much of that
publication's punctuation, suggests that Quince speaks very
haltingly, with a tentativeness that befits his modest,
fastidious, bashful personality.

75 **And**   If.
terribly   Quince means 'terrifyingly', but the more usual
colloquial meaning is unintentionally applicable as well.

77 **shrike**   shriek.

FLUTE   Here, Peter Quince.

QUINCE   Flute, you must take Thisby, on you.   45

FLUTE   What is Thisby? A wand'ring Knight?

QUINCE   It is the Lady, that Pyramus must love.

FLUTE   Nay faith, let not me play a Woman: I have
a Beard coming.

QUINCE   That's all one: you shall play it in a Mask,   50
and you may speak as small as you will.

BOTTOM   And I may hide my Face, let me play Thisby
too. I'll speak in a monstrous little Voice:
Thisne, Thisne.
Ah, Pyramus, my Lover dear, thy Thisby
dear, and Lady dear.   55

QUINCE   No, no: you must play Pyramus. – And Flute,
you Thisby.

BOTTOM   Well, proceed.

QUINCE   Robin Starveling, the Tailor?

STARVELING   Here, Peter Quince.   60

QUINCE   Robin Starveling, you must play Thisby's
Mother. – Tom Snout, the Tinker?

SNOUT   Here, Peter Quince.

QUINCE   You, Pyramus' Father. My self, Thisby's
Father. – Snug, the Joiner, you the Lion's Part.   65
– And I hope here is a Play fitted.

SNUG   Have you the Lion's Part written? Pray you,
if it be, give it me: for I am slow of study.

QUINCE   You may do it, *extempore*: for it is nothing
but roaring.   70

BOTTOM   Let me play the Lion too. I will roar that
I will do any man's Heart good to hear me. I will
roar that I will make the Duke say, 'Let him roar
again, let him roar again.'

QUINCE   And you should do it too terribly, you would   75
fright the Duchess and the Ladies, that they
would shrike: and that were enough to hang
us all.

26

82 **Discretion** (a) prerogative, or (b) sound judgement. The humour in Bottom's phrasing is that, without meaning any disrespect, he presumptuously attributes a lack of judgement to the Duke and his court.

83 **aggravate** make heavier. Of course, Bottom means the opposite of what he says here. Compare Mistress Quickly's malapropism in 2 *Henry IV*, II.iv.175–76.

84 **sucking Dove** Bottom collapses two images from 1 Samuel 7:9, which refers to 'the sucking lamb or harmless dove'.

84–85 **and 'twere** as if it were.

87 **Proper** handsome, well-mannered.

94 **discharge** 'undertake' (line 91), perform. See the note to line 10.

95 **Orange-tawny** tan.

96 **Purple-in-grain** fast-dyed a deep crimson or scarlet colour.

97 **perfit** Bottom's pronunciation of *perfect*.

98 **French Crowns** Quince picks up on Bottom's line about the 'perfit Yellow' (line 97) characteristic of French crowns (gold coins) and alludes to the 'crowns' (bald heads) of those with what was known as the 'French disease' (syphilis).

99 **Bare-fac'd** both (a) beardless, and (b) undisguised.

104 **a ... Town** a mile beyond the city limits. Compare I.i.163–68.

106 **Devises** devices. Entertainments such as plays were often said to be 'devised'. Compare I.i.213.

107 **Bill of Properties** list of stage paraphernalia (what are still referred to as 'props').

110 **obscenely** Bottom probably thinks that the word relates to the seemly (proper) performing of scenes. Later, lines such as V.i.204 will give *obscenely* a humorously ironic pertinence.

110–11 **be perfit** learn your parts, and be able to speak your lines perfectly.

ALL   That would hang us, every Mother's Son.

BOTTOM   I grant you, Friends, if you should fright   80
the Ladies out of their Wits, they would have
no more Discretion but to hang us. But I will
aggravate my Voice so that I will roar you, as
gently as any sucking Dove; I will roar you, and
'twere any Nightingale.   85

QUINCE   You can play no Part but Pyramus: for
Pyramus is a Sweet-fac'd Man; a Proper Man as
one shall see in a Summer's Day; a most lovely
Gentleman-like Man. Therefore you must needs
play Pyramus.   90

BOTTOM   Well; I will undertake it. What Beard were
I best to play in?

QUINCE   Why? what you will.

BOTTOM   I will discharge it in either your Straw-
colour Beard, your Orange-tawny Beard, your   95
Purple-in-grain Beard, or your French-crown-
colour Beard, your perfit Yellow.

QUINCE   Some of your French Crowns have no Hair
at all; and then you will play Bare-fac'd. But
Maisters, here are your Parts. And I am to   100
entreat you, request you, and desire you, to
con them by to morrow Night. And meet me in
the Palace Wood, a Mile without the Town, by
Moonlight. There will we rehearse: for if we
meet in the City, we shall be dogg'd with   105
Company, and our Devises known. In the mean
time, I will draw a Bill of Properties, such as our
Play wants. I pray you fail me not.

BOTTOM   We will meet, and there we may rehearse
most obscenely, and courageously. Take pains, be   110
perfit: adieu.

113 **hold, or cut Bowstrings** apparently an expression from archery
(though it could also refer to the bow and strings of a violin
or other string instrument), probably equivalent to 'fish or cut
bait'. It is used here as an admonition to learn your parts or
be cast out of the company. Bottom's phrasing is another
reminder of the bow-and-arrow imagery that pervades a play
about the ministrations of blind Cupid (see I.i.168–70,
234–41), and it recalls such previous passages as I.i.6–11 and
I.ii.10–11; Bottom's message is to 'hold' your aim 'and so
grow to a Point'.

QUINCE   At the Duke's Oak we meet.
BOTTOM   Enough; hold, or cut Bowstrings.   *Exeunt.*

II.i   This scene take place in the wood outside Athens.

1   **whither wander**   Robin's phrase echoes I.i.180, and it keeps us aware that characters in this comedy are unusually prone to 'wander every where' (line 6). Compare I.ii.46.

2–17   **Over . . . anon**   The verse in this speech shifts between trochaic tetrameter (lines 2–8, 11–13), iambic tetrameter (lines 9–10, 14), and the normal verse mode of iambic pentameter (lines 15–17). Variations of rhymed lines carry us from a childlike mode of nursery rhyme (lines 2–5) through a series of rhymed couplets designed to introduce us to Fairyland (lines 6–15), to a transitional couplet (lines 16–17) that establishes rhymed pentameter couplets as the mode of discourse that will be sustained until the entry of Oberon and Titania in line 60.

3–5   **Thorough**   an archaic spelling of *through*, used here for metrical purposes. In similar fashion, 'Moon's' in line 7 is probably to be pronounced as a two-syllable word (either 'Moo-on's' or 'Moon-es').

4   **Pale**   fence to enclose an area.

7   **Sphere**   Like all celestial bodies, the Moon was once thought to revolve around the Earth by means of a crystalline sphere, or hollow 'orb', from which we derive the word 'orbit'.

9   **dew her Orbs**   This phrase recalls I.i.154–55. The 'Orbs' referred to here are 'fairy rings' on the grass; they mimic the Moon's orb and orb-like shape.

10   **Pensioners**   gentlemen of the royal bodyguard, tall and splendid like the gold-coated cowslips. Spots recalls I.i.110. The 'Spots' on their apparel are ruby-like 'Freckles' (line 13), bestowed as 'Favours' (gifts from the Fairies to give the flowers 'Savours' (sweet fragrances).

16   **Lob**   clumsy bumpkin, suggesting that Robin is a larger and less delicate spirit than the 'Elves' (line 17) accompanying Titania.

20   **passing fell and wrath**   exceedingly fierce and wrathful (angry). The meaning of *passing* here is 'surpassing'.

23   **Changeling**   here pronounced as a three-syllable word. The name *Changeling* usually refers to an imp the Fairies have left in exchange for a stolen human child. In this instance it refers to a human child the Fairies have 'stolen' (line 22).

25   **trace**   traverse, track.

ACT II

Scene 1

Enter a Fairy at one Door, and Robin Goodfellow at another.

ROBIN   How now, Spirit; whither wander you?
FAIRY   Over Hill, over Dale,
      Thorough Bush, thorough Brier,
    Over Park, over Pale,
      Thorough Flood, thorough Fire,   5
    I do wander every where;
    Swifter than the Moon's Sphere;
    And I serve the Fairy Queen,
    To dew her Orbs upon the Green.
    The Cowslips tall her Pensioners be: 10
    In their Gold Coats, Spots you see;
    Those be Rubies, Fairy Favours;
    In those Freckles live their Savours.
  I must go seek some Dewdrops here,
  And hang a Pearl in every Cowslip's Ear.   15
  Farewell, thou Lob of Spirits, I'll be gone;
  Our Queen and all her Elves come here anon.
ROBIN   The King doth keep his Revels here to night;
  Take heed the Queen come not within his Sight,
  For Oberon is passing fell and wrath   20
  Because that she, as her Attendant, hath
  A lovely Boy stolen from an Indian King.
  She never had so sweet a Changeling,
  And jealous Oberon would have the Child,
  Knight of his Train, to trace the Forests wild.   25

26 **perforce** both (a) by force, and (b) of necessity (knowing of Oberon's desire to have him).

29 **spangled Starlight Sheen** the glittering lustre of starlight. This poetic phrase is a wonderful evocation of the special magic of Fairyland.

30 **square** square off, quarrel.

32 **Making** physical makeup, build.

33 **shrewd** cursed (beshrewed), and thus demonically and cleverly mischievous.

36 **Quern** handmill for grinding grain.

37 **bootless** fruitless, for nothing.
    Huswife housewife. The archaic spelling reflects the rustic flavour and pronunciation of the word in this context.

38 **bear no Barm** fail to ferment or produce foam, owing to a lack of yeast.

39 **Mislead Night Wanderers** In this sentence normal grammar would call for *Misleads* here, and for *Skims*, *labours*, and *makes* (twice) in lines 36–38. The Fairy's phrasing echoes lines 1 and 43, and it anticipates the role Robin will play with the 'Night Wanderers' who are coming to the wood.

41 **good Luck** This phrase echoes I.i.221, and line 41 defines the beneficence 'sweet Puck' will bring to Helena and Demetrius, Hermia and Lysander.

44 **jest** tell jokes. Here as elsewhere, *jest* is spelled *ieast* in the early printings. It was probably close to *yeast* in pronunciation, and the playwright seems to have associated jesting with the froth produced by yeast, even the jesting that inhibits 'Barm' (line 38).

48 **Crab** crabapple, often used in hot, spicy punches.

50 **Dewlop** dewlap, folds of skin under the chin. Compare IV.i.125. *Withered* recalls line 1 and I.i.6, 77, 180.

54 **Tailor** Various explanations have been given for this obscure ejaculation; it may simply be what one says after falling on his 'tail'. But since *tail* was a common term for the male member (translating the Latin word *penis*), *Tailor* could also refer to a lustful man.
    Coffe cough (perhaps with play on 'cuff'). In the following line, *loffe* suggests a rustic pronunciation of 'laugh'.

55 **Quire** choir, company.

But she, perforce, withholds the loved Boy,
Crowns him with Flowers, and makes him all her
   Joy;
And now they never meet in Grove or Green,
By Fountain clear, or spangled Starlight Sheen,
But they do square, that all their Elves for fear   30
Creep into Acorn Cups and hide them there.
FAIRY   Either I mistake your Shape and Making quite,
   Or else you are that shrewd and knavish Sprite
   Call'd Robin Goodfellow. Are you not he
   That frights the Maidens of the Villagery,   35
   Skim Milk, and sometimes labour in the Quern,
   And bootless make the breathless Huswife churn,
   And sometime make the Drink to bear no Barm,
   Mislead Night Wanderers, laughing at their Harm?
   Those that Hobgoblin call you, and sweet Puck,   40
   You do their Work, and they shall have good Luck:
   Are not you he?
ROBIN   Thou speakest aright;
   I am that merry Wanderer of the Night.
   I jest to Oberon, and make him smile,
   When I a fat and bean-fed Horse beguile,   45
   Neighing in likeness of a Filly Foal.
   And sometime lurk I in a Gossip's Bowl
   In very likeness of a rosted Crab;
   And when she drinks, against her Lips I bob,
   And on her withered Dewlop pour the Ale.   50
   The wisest Aunt, telling the saddest Tale,
   Sometime for three-foot Stool mistaketh me;
   Then slip I from her Bum, down topples she,
   And Tailor cries, and falls into a Coffe,
   And then the whole Quire hold their Hips and loffe,   55
   And waxen in their Mirth, and neeze, and swear
   A merrier Hour was never wasted there.
   But room, Fairy: here comes Oberon.
FAIRY   And here my Mistress. Would that he were
   gone.

60   **Ill met . . . Titania** Oberson is saying that it is regrettable ('ill')
that he and Titania have happened upon each other at night:
because of their quarrel, they have not been sleeping together
of late. In this scene Oberon is usually designated by name
rather than as 'King of Fairies'; Titania (Oberon's Queen of
Fairies) is usually labelled 'Queen' in the speech headings.
'Robin' is identified primarily as 'Puck' after line 154.

61   **Fairy, skip hence** It is not clear to whom Titania's line is
addressed: to Oberon, to a fairy, or to herself. Many editors
emend to *Fairies*.

66   **Corin** a conventional name, like Phillida (line 68), from
pastoral poetry about shepherds and shepherdesses.

67   **Pipes of Corn** pipes made of oat stalks. Here as elsewhere *Corn*
refers to various grains, usually oats or wheat, not sweetcorn
(maize).

69   **farthest Steppe** farthest step or utmost reach of India. Titania is
probably not using *Steppe* in the sense now limited to the
plains of central Asia.

71   **buskin'd** wearing high-soled hunting boots.

75   **Glaunce at my Credit** object to my favour. The punctuation for
lines 74–76 follows that of the Quarto. Shakespeare
frequently divides a question into its interrogative and
indicative components, leaving an incomplete sentence after
the question mark.

78–80 **Perigenia . . . Antiopa** Shakespeare adapts this material from
Plutarch's 'Life of Theseus', where he'd have read that the
famous warrior had loved and left four women: Perigouna,
Aegles, Ariadne, and Antiopa. He changes two of the names
and suggests that it was 'with fair Eagles' that Theseus
betrayed Ariadne and Antiopa.

82   **the Middle Summer's Spring** the beginning of midsummer (that
is, the summer solstice in late June).

84   **paved Fountain** spring water flowing over a 'pavement' of
pebbles.

85   **Margent** margin, shore.

87   **Brawls** quarrels, but with a play on the name of a dance (from
the French word *bransle*) in which participants held hands in
'Ringlets' (small rings), as described in line 86.

*Enter the King of Fairies, at one Door, with his Train; and the
Queen, at another, with hers.*

OBERON   Ill met by Moonlight, proud Titania.   60
QUEEN   What, jealous Oberon? Fairy, skip hence.
  I have forsworn his Bed and Company.
OBERON   Tarry, rash Wanton: am not I thy Lord?
QUEEN   Then I must be thy Lady. But I know
  When thou hast stolen away from Fairy Land   65
  And in the shape of Corin sat all Day
  Playing on Pipes of Corn and versing Love
  To amorous Phillida. Why art thou here
  Come from the farthest Steppe of India,
  But that, forsooth, the bouncing Amazon,   70
  Your buskin'd Mistress and your Warrior Love,
  To Theseus must be wedded; and you come
  To give their Bed Joy and Prosperity.
OBERON   How canst thou thus, for Shame, Titania,
  Glaunce at my Credit with Hippolyta?   75
  Knowing I know thy Love to Theseus.
  Didst not thou lead him through the glimmering
    Night
  From Perigenia, whom he ravished,
  And make him, with fair Eagles, break his Faith
  With Ariadne and Antiopa?   80
QUEEN   These are the forgeries of Jealousy;
  And never since the Middle Summer's Spring
  Met we on Hill, in Dale, Forest, or Mead,
  By paved Fountain or by rushy Brook,
  Or in the beached Margent of the Sea,   85
  To daunce our Ringlets to the whistling Wind,
  But with thy Brawls thou hast disturb'd our
    Sport.
  Therefore the Winds, piping to us in vain,
  As in Revenge have suck'd up from the Sea
  Contagious Fogs, which, falling in the Land,   90

91 **pelting** paltry or petty.

92 **Continents** banks (literally, containers). *Yoke* (line 93) recalls I.i.81.

96 **Fold** pen for enclosing sheep.

97 **Murrion Flock** sheep dead from murrain, a fatal disease.

98 **Nine-Men's-Morris** a nine-pin game played in grooves carved from turf. Here the reference is to the grooved turf.

99 **queint Mazes** quaint and intricate turf arrangements, now overgrown by the green made 'wanton' (excessively abundant) by too much moisture. *Wanton* echoes line 63.

101 **humane** human. Compare II.ii.63.

105 **rheumatic** here accented on the first syllable. The diseases caused by the high tides, rains, and floods are characterised by fluid ('rheum') and are hence called 'rheumatic'.

106 **Distemperature** imbalance of the elements, both in the atmosphere and in the human body.

109 **Hiems'** Winter personified, from Latin *hiemalis*.

110 **Chaplet** wreath or garland.

112 **childing** child-bearing, fruitful.
change exchange.

113 **wonted Liveries** accustomed apparel. Compare I.i.70.
mazed both astonished, and bewildered (as in a maze).

114 **Increase** both (a) 'Progeny' (line 115), offspring, and (b) extension beyond their normal 'Continents' (line 92).

117 **Original** originators.

118 **amend** correct, restore.

119 **cross** annoy, frustrate. Compare I.i.136, 150.

121 **Henchman** attendant, squire.

123 **Vot'ress** member; one who has taken vows.

125 **gossip'd** As in line 47, this word refers primarily to idle chatter. But here it also carried a hint of its original sense. Gossips (from 'God sibs') were godparents, baptismal sponsors, who committed themselves to be surrogate guardians of their godchildren.

Hath every pelting River made so proud
That they have overborne their Continents.
The Ox hath therefore stretch'd his Yoke in vain,
The Ploughman lost his Sweat, and the green Corn
Hath rotted ere his Youth attain'd a Beard;   95
The Fold stands empty in the drowned Field,
And Crows are fatted with the Murrion Flock.
The Nine-Men's-Morris is fill'd up with Mud,
And the queint Mazes in the wanton Green,
For lack of Tread, are undistinguishable.   100
The humane Mortals want their Winter here;
No Night is now with Hymn or Carol blest.
Therefore the Moon (the Governess of Floods),
Pale in her Anger, washes all the Air
That rheumatic Diseases do abound.   105
And thorough this Distemperature we see
The Seasons alter: hoary-headed Frosts
Fall in the fresh Lap of the crimson Rose,
And on old Hiems' Chin and icy Crown
An odorous Chaplet of sweet Summer Buds   110
Is as in Mockery set. The Spring, the Summer,
The childing Autumn, angry Winter change
Their wonted Liveries; and the mazed World
By their Increase now knows not which is which.
And this same Progeny of Evils comes   115
From our Debate, from our Dissension:
We are their Parents and Original.

OBERON   Do you amend it then: it lies in you.
Why should Titania cross her Oberon?
I do but beg a little Changeling Boy   120
To be my Henchman.

QUEEN   Set your Heart at rest:
The Fairy Land buys not the Child of me.
His Mother was a Vot'ress of my Order,
And in the spiced Indian Air by Night
Full often hath she gossip'd by my side   125

126 **Neptune's yellow Sands** the beach belonging to the God of the Sea.

127 **Traders** trading ships filled with merchandise.
   Flood waters, sea.

129 **big-bellied** Just as the mother of the 'Changeling Boy' (line 120) conceived and grew big-bellied with him, so the sails of the ships grow pregnant with the 'wanton' (erotically playful) wind. *Wanton* echoes line 99.

140 **patiently** Here pronounced as a four-syllable word, with the first and third syllables stressed; *in* is then combined with *daunce* to yield the metre: 'If yoú/wĭll pá/tĭent/lў daúnce 'n/oŭr Roúnd'. *Round* (roundel) recalls 'Ringlets' (line 86).

142 **shun** avoid.
   spare leave undisturbed.

145 **chide downright** quarrel without restraint.

146 **Thou shalt not** 'Go' is understood to follow 'not'.

149 **Since** when.

151 **dulcet** sweet. *Hermonious* (harmonious) plays on 'her' and 'moan'.

153 **madly** crazily, dotingly.

157 **certain** both (a) particular, and (b) fixed, stable, accurate.

And sat with me on Neptune's yellow Sands
Marking th' embarked Traders on the Flood,
When we have laugh'd to see the Sails conceive
And grow big-bellied with the wanton Wind,
Which she with pretty and with swimming Gait   130
Following (her Womb then rich with my young
    Squire)
Would imitate, and sail upon the Land
To fetch me Trifles and return again
As from a Voyage, rich with Marchandise.
But she, being mortal, of that Boy did die,   135
And for her sake do I rear up her Boy,
And for her sake I will not part with him.
OBERON   How long within this Wood intend you stay?
QUEEN   Perchaunce till after Theseus' Wedding Day.
    If you will patiently daunce in our Round   140
    And see our Moonlight Revels, go with us;
    If not, shun me, and I will spare your Haunts.
OBERON   Give me that Boy, and I will go with thee.
QUEEN   Not for thy Fairy Kingdom. – Fairies, away.
    We shall chide downright if I longer stay.   145
                          Exeunt [*Titania and her Train*].
OBERON   Well: go thy way. Thou shalt not from this
    Grove
Till I torment thee for this Injury.
– My gentle Puck, come hither. Thou rememb'rest
Since once I sat upon a Promontory
And heard a Mermaid on a Dolphin's Back   150
Uttering such dulcet and hermonious Breath
That the rude Sea grew civil at her Song
And certain Stars shot madly from their Spheres
To hear the Seamaid's Music?
PUCK   I remember.
OBERON   That very Time I saw (but thou couldst not),   155
    Flying between the cold Moon and the Earth,
    Cupid, all arm'd. A certain Aim he took

158 **Vestal** Virgin; originally one consecrated to the Goddess of the Hearth (Vestia in Roman mythology, Hestia in Greek mythology). The 'fair Vestal throned by the West' is usually thought to be a complimentary allusion to Queen Elizabeth, who refused to marry. Compare I.i.74–78, a passage that would also have reminded Elizabethans of their 'Thrice blessed' Queen.

160 **As** as if.

161 **I might see** I was able to see.

161– **But . . . fell** Diana's power to protect the chastity of her
65 'Vot'ress' (disciple) caused Cupid's 'fiery Shaft' to miss its mark and leave the would-be victim 'Fancy-free' (free of Love's infatuation). *Fancy* recalls I.i.155.

163 **chast** both (a) chaste, and (b) chas'd, hotly pursued, like the Queen the Moon treasures as her 'fair Vestal'. This passage looks forward to III.i.202–6.

165 **Bolt** arrow.

166 **little Western Flower** probably a pansy.

167 **Purple** blood-red, crimson. Compare I.ii.94–97.

171 **or . . . or** either . . . or.
madly dote Oberon's phrase recalls I.i.108–10.

174 **Leviathan** Sea monster, usually assumed to be a whale, and referred to in Job 41:1 and in Psalms 74:15 and 124:26.

178 **Liquor** liquid.

181 **medling** both (a) meddling, interfering, and (b) wanton (by association with the 'medler' or 'medlar', a fruit best eaten when overripe and proverbially associated with erotic indulgence (including self-meddling). Compare *Romeo and Juliet*, II.i.34–38; *As You Like It*, III.ii.106–30; *Troilus and Cressida*, I.i.13–14, 67–70, 87–88; *Coriolanus*, IV.v.30–34; and *Timon of Athens*, IV.iii.300–5.

186 **I am Invisible** Some action may be indicated here. Perhaps Oberon folds his cape about him in a gesture of 'invisibility', or he may simply retire to an unobtrusive position on the stage. On the other hand, Oberon's words may simply be a way of informing the audience that Fairies cannot normally be perceived by mere mortals. What Bottom experiences later in the play is a 'most rare Vision' (IV.i.207) in a quite literal sense.

At a fair Vestal throned by the West
And loos'd his Love-shaft smartly from his Bow
As it should pierce a hundred thousand Hearts: 160
But I might see young Cupid's fiery Shaft
Quench'd in the chast Beams of the wat'ry Moon,
And the imperial Vot'ress passed on
In Maiden Meditation, Fancy-free.
Yet mark'd I where the Bolt of Cupid fell: 165
It fell upon a little Western Flower,
Before Milk-white, now Purple with Love's Wound,
And Maidens call it Love-in-Idleness.
Fetch me that Flow'r; the Herb I shew'd thee
    once.
The Juice of it, on sleeping Eyelids laid,   170
Will make or Man or Woman madly dote
Upon the next live Creature that it sees.
Fetch me this Herb, and be thou here again
Ere the Leviathan can swim a League.

PUCK   I'll put a Girdle round about the Earth   175
In forty Minutes.   [*Exit.*]

OBERON   Having once this Juice,
I'll watch Titania when she is asleep
And drop the Liquor of it in her Eyes;
The next thing then she, waking, looks upon
(Be it on Lion, Bear, or Wolf, or Bull,   180
Or medling Monkey, or on busy Ape)
She shall pursue it with the Soul of Love.
And ere I take this Charm from off her Sight
(As I can take it with another Herb),
I'll make her render up her Page to me.   185
But who comes here? I am Invisible,
And I will overhear their Conference.

Enter Demetrius, Helena following him.

DEMETRIUS   I love thee not, therefore pursue me not.

190 **stay ... stayeth** Most editors emend these words to *slay* and *slayeth*. If Demetrius enters with his sword drawn (which would be consistent with Helena's first words, in line 195), it may be that he does have murder on his mind. But *stay/stayeth* (arrest, stop) could carry that implication as well as their more normal, less severe meanings.

192 **wodde** wood (a variant spelling the Quarto employs here to distinguish it from the *Wood* that means 'forest'); frenzied, madly frantic.

195 **Adamant** both (a) loadstone or magnet, and (b) a metal or stone of consummate hardness.

196 **draw not Iron** attract not base metal. Helena puns on a phrase that could also refer to drawing a sword to 'stay' an adversary.

197 **true as Steel** proverbial phrase for faithfulness. Helena seems to be saying that, unlike *Iron* (line 196), which is associated with hard-heartedness, she represents a metal of superior mettle.

199 **speak you fair** 'entice you' by praising your beauty and charm.

205 **spurn** kick.

206 **loose** both (a) release, unleash, and (b) lose, discard. Compare I.i.114.

209 **Respect** esteem. Compare line 224 and I.i.160.

214 **impeach** call into question, sully. *Modesty* recalls I.i.60.

218 **Desert** deserted. *Ill Counsel* here means 'ill-advised (unwise) setting'. But *Ill* also suggests that this place harbours evil dangers.

220 **Your Virtue is my Privilege** Your virtue is what gives me the right to be here without endangering my virginity or impeaching my reputation.
  for that because.

Where is Lysander, and fair Hermia?
The one I'll stay; the other stayeth me.   190
Thou toldst me they were stol'n unto this Wood;
And here am I, and wodde, within this Wood,
Because I cannot meet my Hermia.
Hence, get thee gone, and follow me no more.

HELENA   You draw me, you hard-hearted Adamant,   195
But yet you draw not Iron, for my Heart
Is true as Steel. Leave you your power to draw,
And I shall have no power to follow you.

DEMETRIUS   Do I entice you? Do I speak you fair?
Or rather do I not in plainest Truth   200
Tell you I do not, nor I cannot, love you?

HELENA   And even for that do I love you the more.
I am your Spaniel; and Demetrius,
The more you beat me I will fawn on you.
Use me but as your Spaniel: spurn me, strike me,   205
Neglect me, loose me; only give me leave,
Unworthy as I am, to follow you.
What worse Place can I beg in your Love
(And yet a Place of high Respect with me)
Than to be used as you use your Dog?   210

DEMETRIUS   Tempt not too much the Hatred of my
    Spirit;
For I am Sick when I do look on thee.

HELENA   And I am Sick when I look not on you.

DEMETRIUS   You do impeach your Modesty too much,
To leave the City and commit your self   215
Into the Hands of one that loves you not:
To trust the Opportunity of Night,
And the Ill Counsel of a Desert Place,
With the rich Worth of your Virginity.

HELENA   Your Virtue is my Privilege: for that   220
It is not Night when I do see your Face.
Therefore I think I am not in the Night,
Nor doth this Wood lack Worlds of Company,

227   **Brakes** thickets.

230– **The Story shall be chaung'd . . . and Valour flies** In Book I of
34   his *Metamorphoses* Ovid describes how the nymph Daphne,
      pursued by Apollo, was rescued from his embraces by being
      transformed into a laurel. Helena would reverse or exchange
      ('change', line 230) the normal roles of male ('Valour') and
      female ('Cowardice'). She notes that 'speed' is 'bootless'
      (useless) when the pursued turns around and gives chase to
      the pursuer. *Chaung'd* recalls lines 23, 112, and I.i.181–91.

232   **Griffin** a mythological creature combining the body and hind
      legs of a lion, and the head, wings, and front legs of an eagle.
      Hind female deer. *Bootless* (line 233) echoes line 37.

235   **Questions** 'Questions' (from Latin *quaestio*) were points at
      issue in formal debates. Demetrius says he has no time for
      Helena's exercises in forensic ingenuity. *Stay* (remain for)
      recalls lines 138, 190.

238   **I** Helena's primary meaning is 'Ay' (yes), but 'I' fits the context
      too. Compare line 248.

240   **Your Wrongs** a reminder that Demetrius, having been
      betrothed to Helena, has humiliated her and, by extension,
      women generally ('set a Scandal on my Sex'). One of Helena's
      points is that, like Lysander, she is seeking merely to
      'prosecute' her 'Right' (I.i.105) as one to whom love and
      marriage have been solemnly vowed (compare I.i.28–29). In a
      way that parallels the Helena of *All's Well That Ends Well*,
      she considers Demetrius her betrothed, her rightful husband.

243   **make . . . Hell** Helena's words recall what she said in
      I.i.246–51. Compare I.i.140.

244   **upon the Hand** as a victim of the sword. Helena continues the
      duelling imagery of lines 195–97, 241.

247   **Wanderer** This epithet echoes lines 1, 6, 43.

250   **Oxlips** flowers of the primrose family.

251   **Woodbine** either honeysuckle or a related vine.

252   **Musk-roses** wild roses with fragrant white flowers.
      Eglantine sweet-brier, a type of wild rose with pink flowers
      and scented leaves.

For you, in my Respect, are all the World.
Then how can it be said I am alone   225
When all the World is here to look on me?
DEMETRIUS   I'll run from thee, and hide me in the
   Brakes,
And leave thee to the mercy of wild Beasts.
HELENA   The wildest hath not such a Heart as you.
Run when you will, the Story shall be chaung'd: 230
Apollo flies and Daphne holds the Chase;
The Dove pursue the Griffin; the mild Hind
Makes speed to catch the Tiger. Bootless speed,
When Cowardice pursues and Valour flies.
DEMETRIUS   I will not stay thy Questions. Let me go: 235
Or if thou follow me, do not believe
But I shall do thee Mischief in the Wood.
HELENA   I, in the Temple, in the Town, the Field,
You do me Mischief. Fie, Demetrius.
Your Wrongs do set a Scandal on my Sex: 240
We cannot fight for Love as Men may do;
We should be woo'd, and were not made to woo.
                              [*Exit Demetrius.*]
I'll follow thee and make a Heaven of Hell,
To die upon the Hand I love so well.   *Exit.*
OBERON   Fare thee well, Nymph. Ere he do leave this
   Grove   245
Thou shalt fly him, and he shall seek thy Love.

                        Enter Puck.

– Hast thou the Flower there? Welcome, Wanderer.
PUCK   Ay, there it is.
OBERON   I pray thee give it me.
I know a Bank where the wild Thyme blows,
Where Oxlips and the nodding Violet grows,   250
Quite overcanopi'd with luscious Woodbine,
With sweet Musk-roses and with Eglantine.

253 **sometime of the Night** sometimes at night.

255 **throws** sheds.
enamell'd hard and shiny

256 **Weed** garment.

258 **hateful Phantasies** loathsome fantasies (desires or imaginings).

266 **fond on** infatuated with, doting upon. Lines 259–60 echo lines 169–85.

II.ii The scene shifts to Titania's bower in the woods.

1 **Roundel** a circular dance; from the French *rondele*. Compare II.i.86, 140.

3 **Cankers** canker-worms; caterpillars, plant-eating larvae.

4 **Reremice** bats.

6 **clamorous** disturbingly noisy. Compare *Macbeth*, I.vii.78, II.iii.65–66.

7 **queint** quaint; delicate, dainty.

8 **Offices** posts, the duties just assigned.

9 s.h. There is no speech heading at this point in the Quarto and Folio texts. The same is true for lines 13, 24. Like other modern editions, this one supplies what appear to be the most likely assignments.
double forked. *Snakes* echoes II.i.253–56.

There sleeps Titania sometime of the Night,
Lull'd in these Flowers with Daunces and Delight;
And there the Snake throws her enamell'd Skin,   255
Weed wide enough to wrap a Fairy in.
And with the Juice of this I'll streak her Eyes,
And make her full of hateful Phantasies.
Take thou some of it and seek through this Grove:
A sweet Athenian Lady is in love   260
With a disdainful Youth; anoint his Eyes,
But do it when the next thing he espies
May be the Lady. Thou shalt know the Man
By the Athenian Garments he hath on.
Effect it with some Care, that he may prove   265
More fond on her than she upon her Love.
And look thou meet me ere the first Cock crow.
PUCK   Fear not, my Lord; your Servant shall do so.

                                                    Exeunt.

Scene 2

Enter Titania, Queen of Fairies, with her Train.

QUEEN   Come now, a Roundel, and a Fairy Song;
   Then for the third part of a Minute hence,
   Some to kill Cankers in the Musk-rose Buds,
   Some war with Reremice for their leath'ren Wings
   To make my small Elves Coats, and some keep back   5
   The clamorous Owl that nightly hoots and wonders
   At our queint Spirits. Sing me now asleep,
   Then to your Offices, and let me rest.

Fairies sing.

[1 FAIRY]   You spotted Snakes, with double Tongue,

48

11   **Newts and Blindworms**   Now known to be harmless, these tiny
      creatures were thought to be venomous in Shakespeare's time.

13   **Philomele**   nightingale personified. In Book VI of Ovid's
      Metamorphoses Philomela is violated by her sister Progne's
      husband, Tereus, who cuts out her tongue so that she will not
      disclose his crime. Eventually, to escape death at his hands,
      she is metamorphosed into a nightingale.

14   **Sing in**   literally, in-chant. Compare *Macbeth*, IV.i.41–43.

17   **Charm**   evil spell, a 'wrong' (line 11) even more to be warded
      off than whatever the Newt or Hedgehog might do.

18   **nigh**   near.

21   **long-legg'd Spinners**   daddy-longlegs, in all probability.

32   **One aloof, stand Sentinel**   How this command is to be carried
      out is a matter of interpretation for each director. In
      productions where a 'Sentinel' is left near Titania, Oberon
      must either elude him, remove him, render him ineffectual, or
      win him over as an ally.

33–34 **what . . . take**   As Oberon speaks these words, he squeezes onto
      Titania's eyelids the juice he referred to in II.i.165–85,
      249–64. Oberon's rhyming trochaic tetrameters resemble the
      verse employed in other places by the inhabitants of
      Fairyland. Compare II.i.2–13; II.ii.72–89; III.ii.102–21,
      396–99; IV.i.96–105; and V.i.375–442.

36   **Ounce**   lynx.

37   **Pard**   panther or leopard.

  Thorny Hedgehogs, be not seen;   10
  Newts and Blindworms, do not wrong;
   Come not near our Fairy Queen.
[CHORUS] Philomele, with Melody,
   Sing in our sweet Lullaby,
  Lulla, lulla, Lullaby; lulla, lulla, Lullaby; 15
    Never Harm,
     Nor Spell, nor Charm,
   Come our lovely Lady nigh.
   So good night, with Lullaby.
1 FAIRY Weaving Spiders, come not here;   20
   Hence you long-legg'd Spinners,
    hence;
   Beetles black, approach not near;
    Worm nor Snail, do no offense.
[CHORUS] Philomele, with Melody,
   Sing in our sweet Lullaby,   25
  Lulla, lulla, Lullaby; lulla, lulla, Lullaby;
    Never Harm,
     Nor Spell, nor Charm,
   Come our lovely Lady nigh.
   So good night, with Lullaby.   30
2 FAIRY Hence away: now all is well.
   One aloof, stand Sentinel.   *She sleeps.*
          [*Exeunt Fairies.*]

Enter Oberon.

OBERON What thou seest when thou dost wake,
  Do it for thy true Love take;
  Love and languish for his sake.   35
  Be it Ounce, or Cat, or Bear,
  Pard, or Boar with bristled Hair
  In thy Eye that shall appear,
  When thou wak'st, it is thy Dear.
  Wake when some Vile Thing is near. [*Exit.*] 40

41   **wand'ring** Lysander's phrasing echoes II.i.246.

42   **troth** truth; truthfully, faithfully.

48   **Troth** pledge of fidelity, betrothal.

49   **god** good (for which *god* was a variant form in Shakespeare's time). Compare I.i.47, where Theseus tells Hermia that her 'Father should be as a God' to her.

52   **Love's Conference** the kind of conferring, or conversation, that only lovers know. *Conference* recalls II.i.187.

55   **interchained** chained together. Compare 'interchang'd Love-tokens' (I.i.29).

57   **Bed-room** sleeping space.

58   **lying ... lie** Lysander puns ('riddles', line 59) on two meanings of *lie*: (a) lie down, and (b) be untruthful or unfaithful.

59   **prettily** wittily, charmingly.

60   **beshrew** condemn, curse. Compare II.i.33.

63   **humane Modesty** the modesty befitting a gracious human being. The usual spelling for *human* in Shakespeare's time was *humane*, and it encompassed the connotations we now associate with both words. Compare II.i.110.

65   **Maid** virgin. Since *Maid* was not completely gender-specific, it could here refer to Lysander as well as to Hermia. Compare *Twelfth Night*, V.i.266, where Sebastian tells Lady Olivia that she is 'betroth'd both to a Maid and Man'.

Enter Lysander and Hermia.

LYSANDER   Fair Love, you faint with wand'ring in the
   Wood;
   And to speak troth, I have forgot our way.
   We'll rest us, Hermia, if you think it good,
   And tarry for the Comfort of the Day.
HERMIA   Be't so, Lysander. Find you out a Bed;   45
   For I upon this Bank will rest my Head.
LYSANDER   One Turf shall serve as Pillow for us
   both:
   One Heart, one Bed, two Bosoms, and one Troth.
HERMIA   Nay, god Lysander. For my sake, my Dear,
   Lie further off yet; do not lie so near.   50
LYSANDER   O take the Sense, Sweet, of my Innocence;
   Love takes the Meaning in Love's Conference.
   I mean that my Heart unto yours is knit,
   So that but one Heart we can make of it.
   Two Bosoms interchained with an Oath: 55
   So then two Bosoms and a single Troth.
   Then by your side no Bed-room me deny;
   For lying so, Hermia, I do not lie.
HERMIA   Lysander riddles very prettily;
   Now much beshrew my Manners and my Pride,   60
   If Hermia meant to say Lysander lied.
   But gentle Friend, for Love and Courtesy,
   Lie further off in humane Modesty:
   Such Separation as may well be said
   Becomes a virtuous Bachelor and a Maid,   65
   So far be distant, and good night, sweet Friend;
   Thy Love ne'er alter till thy sweet Life end.
LYSANDER   Amen, amen, to that fair Prayer, say I,
   And then end Life when I end Loyalty.
   Here is my Bed; Sleep give thee all his Rest.   70
HERMIA   With half that Wish the Wisher's Eyes be
   presst.   *They sleep.*

74   **approve**   prove, demonstrate.

77   **Weeds of Athens**   Athenian apparel. *Weed* recalls II.i.256.

81   **dank**   moist.

83   **Kill-courtesy**   murderer of courtesy; similar to the more
      familiar *killjoy*.

84   **Churl**   surly boor. *Charm* echoes line 17.

85   **owe**   own, possess. As he speaks lines 84–88 Puck anoints
      Lysander's eyes with the love-potion.

90   **Stay**   Helena's verb recalls II.i.190, 235.

91   **charge**   order, command.

92   **darkling**   in the dark.

94   **fond**   both (a) foolish, and (b) inspired by love. Compare
      II.i.266.

95   **Grace**   benefit, reward; answer to 'Prayer'.

97   **attractive**   literally, magnetic. Helena's imagery recalls
      II.i.195–98, and I.i.181–201.

Enter Puck.

PUCK Through the Forest have I gone,
But Athenian found I none
On whose Eyes I might approve
This Flower's force in stirring Love.   75
Night and Silence. Who is here?
Weeds of Athens he doth wear:
This is he, my Master said,
Despised the Athenian Maid.
And here the Maiden, sleeping sound,   80
On the dank and dirty Ground.
Pretty Soul, she durst not lie
Near this Lack-love, this Kill-courtesy.
Churl, upon thy Eyes I throw
All the power this Charm doth owe;   85
When thou wak'st, let Love forbid
Sleep his Seat on thy Eyelid.
So awake when I am gone,
For I must now to Oberon.   *Exit.*

Enter Demetrius and Helena running.

HELENA   Stay, though thou kill me, sweet Demetrius.   90
DEMETRIUS   I charge thee hence, and do not haunt
me thus.
HELENA   O wilt thou darkling leave me? Do not so.
DEMETRIUS   Stay on thy peril; I alone will go.   *Exit.*
HELENA   O, I am out of Breath: in this fond Chase
The more my Prayer, the lesser is my Grace.   95
Happy is Hermia, wheresoe'er she lies,
For she hath blessed and attractive Eyes.
How came her Eyes so bright? Not with salt Tears;
If so, my Eyes are oft'ner wash'd than hers.
No, no, I am as ugly as a Bear,   100
For Beasts that meet me run away for Fear.

103　　**fly**　flee. Compare I.i.202–3. *Monster* echoes I.ii.53.

104　　**dissembling**　falsifying, deceiving; literally, disfiguring (compare
　　　　I.i.51).
　　　　Glass　mirror. This word recalls I.i.211.

105　　**compare with**　try to become a peer of or rival to.
　　　　sphery Eyne　celestial eyes (by association with the planetary
　　　　and astral spheres).

110–　**Transparent . . . Heart**　Lysander says that by allowing him to
11　　　see Helena's heart as if her bosom were transparent, Nature
　　　　takes on powers normally reserved for Art's improvements on
　　　　Nature. *Shews* can mean either (a) shows, displays, or (b)
　　　　eschews, scorns. *Art* recalls I.i.192–93. *Bosom* echoes lines
　　　　55–56.

120　　**Raven for a Dove**　The dove, a white bird, was associated with
　　　　love, grace, and beauty; the raven, a black bird, was
　　　　associated with hatred, vengeance, and ugliness.

121　　**Will**　The will was the seat of volition or intention; it could be
　　　　guided ('sway'd') either by the reason or by the emotions and
　　　　passions. Lysander, whose will has just been altered by Puck's
　　　　potion, is certain that his change of heart is completely
　　　　rational. *Sway'd* recalls I.i.193, and Lysander's speech as a
　　　　whole echoes Helena's in I.i.234–45. Ironically, when
　　　　Lysander thinks his 'Will' is most 'sway'd' (ruled) by
　　　　'Reason', it is actually being 'sway'd' (thrown off balance) by
　　　　an irrational charm.

123　　**Season**　the end of their growing season.

125　　**And touching . . . Skill**　and arriving now at the apex of that
　　　　skill (the 'Art' of 'Reason') that distinguishes humans from
　　　　creatures lower in the chain of life. *Humane* echoes line 63.
　　　　Point recalls I.ii.10. Lysander believes he finally knows what it
　　　　means to 'grow to a Point'.

126　　**Marshal**　the officer who arranged ceremonial events and saw
　　　　that participants were escorted to their proper places.

127　　**o'erlook**　look or read over.

128　　**Love's richest Book**　In *Love's Labour's Lost*, IV.iii.290–366,
　　　　Berowne too describes 'Women's Eyes' as 'the Ground, the
　　　　Books, the Academs, / From whence doth spring the true
　　　　Promethean Fire'.

134　　**flout**　deride, disdain (line 136, echoing II.i.261).

Therefore no Marvel though Demetrius
Do as a Monster fly my Presence thus.
What wicked and dissembling Glass of mine
Made me compare with Hermia's sphery Eyne!   105
But who is here? Lysander, on the Ground?
Dead or asleep? I see no Blood, no Wound.
– Lysander, if you live, good Sir, awake.

LYSANDER   And run through Fire I will for thy sweet
    sake.
Transparent Helena, Nature shews Art   110
That through thy Bosom makes me see thy Heart.
Where is Demetrius? O how fit a Word
Is that Vile Name to perish on my Sword!

HELENA   Do not say so, Lysander, say not so.
What though he love your Hermia? Lord, what
    though?   115
Yet Hermia still loves you: then be content.

LYSANDER   Content with Hermia? No, I do repent
The tedious Minutes I with her have spent.
Not Hermia but Helena I love:
Who will not change a Raven for a Dove?   120
The Will of Man is by his Reason sway'd,
And Reason says you are the worthier Maid.
Things Growing are not ripe until their Season;
So I, being Young, till now ripe not to Reason.
And touching now the Point of Humane Skill,   125
Reason becomes the Marshal to my Will
And leads me to your Eyes, where I o'erlook
Love's Stories, written in Love's richest Book.

HELENA   Wherefore was I to this Mockery borne?
When at your Hands did I deserve this Scorn?   130
Is't not enough, is't not enough, Young Man,
That I did never, no nor never can,
Deserve a sweet Look from Demetrius' Eye,
But you must flout my Insufficiency?

135   **Good troth . . . good sooth** Both expressions mean *truly* in this context.

137   **Perforce** of necessity. Compare II.i.26.

138   **I thought you Lord . . . Gentleness** Here *Lord* means 'master'. *Lord* recalls I.i.79–82.

140   **abus'd** subjected to deceitful dealings; both deceived and misused.

143   **Surfeit** superfluity, excess. Often *Surfeit* refers to the nausea and other disorders that result from overindulgence, and that sense seems to be implicit in line 147.

145   **Heresies** erroneous beliefs or tenets of faith.

155   **Serpent** venomous snake; also the form that Satan took in the Garden of Eden to tempt Eve (Genesis 3:1). As Hermia speaks lines 151–52 she is crying out during a nightmare. With line 153 she stirs into consciousness.
      eat ate (and so pronounced).

157   **remov'd** departed.

159   **and if** if.

160   **Speak, of all Loves** Hermia invokes Lysander as her symbol of the greatest of all loves. Here *of all Loves* means 'for the sake of the love that inspires all true lovers'.

Good troth you do me wrong, good sooth you do,   135
In such disdainful manner me to woo.
But fare you well. Perforce I must confess
I thought you Lord of more true Gentleness.
O, that a Lady of one Man refus'd
Should of another therefore be abus'd!   *Exit.*   140
LYSANDER   She sees not Hermia. — Hermia, sleep
    thou there,
And never mayst thou come Lysander near:
For as a Surfeit of the Sweetest Things
The deepest Loathing to the Stomach brings,
Or as the Heresies that men do leave   145
Are hated most of those they did deceive,
So thou, my Surfeit and my Heresy,
Of all be hated, but the most of me.
— And all my Powers, address your Love and Might
To honour Helen, and to be her Knight.   *Exit.*   150
HERMIA   Help me, Lysander, help me: do thy best
To pluck this crawling Serpent from my Breast.
Ay me, for pity. What a Dream was here?
Lysander, look how I do quake with Fear.
Me thought a Serpent eat my Heart away,   155
And you sat smiling at his cruel Prey.
Lysander. What, remov'd? Lysander, Lord.
What, out of Hearing gone? No Sound, no Word?
Alack, where are you? Speak, and if you hear;
Speak, of all Loves. I swoon almost with fear.   160
No, then I well perceive you are not nigh;
Either Death or you I'll find immediately.
                                    Exit.

58

III.i   As we know from the last time we saw the rustics ('Clowns'),
         this scene takes place at the Duke's Oak in the wood outside
         Athens.

2   **Pat, pat**   an expression equivalent to 'right on the dot'.
         marvailes   marvellous.

3   **Green Plot**   Quince probably refers to an open grassy area. But
         'Plot' is also a theatrical term for an outline of the action of a
         play.

4–5   **Tiring House**   literally, attiring house, the place for actors to
         don and change costumes. *Brake* (thicket) echoes II.i.227.

8   **bully**   a term of endearment, comparable to 'brother' or
         'valiant'.

11   **draw**   This word recalls II.i.195–98.

12   **abide**   bear, tolerate.

13   **Berlakin**   By our Ladykin, a mild oath originally referring to
         Our Lady the Virgin Mary.
         parlous   perilous, frightful.

16   **Devise**   device (as in I.ii.106).

17–18   **let the Prologue seem to say**   Bottom's phrasing ('seem to say')
         is another comic illustration of his inexperience with the
         conventions of theatrical representation, or 'seeming'.

24   **eight and six**   lines alternating between eight and six syllables
         each, the usual form for ballad meter.

26   **eight and eight**   lines of eight syllables or four metrical feet
         (tetrameter lines). 'To déw / hěr Orbs / ǔp òn / thě Gréen'
         (II.i.9) is an example of a line in iambic tetrameter. As it
         happens, Quince's Prologue (V.i.108 and following) actually
         turns out to be a lame version of iambic pentameter (the same
         five-foot verse form Shakespeare normally uses for dramatic
         dialogue).

ACT III

Scene 1

Enter the Clowns.

BOTTOM   Are we all met?

QUINCE   Pat, pat; and here's a marvailes convenient
place for our Rehearsal. This Green Plot shall
be our Stage, this Hawthorn Brake our Tiring
House, and we will do it in Action as we will   5
do it before the Duke.

BOTTOM   Peter Quince?

QUINCE   What sayest thou, bully Bottom?

BOTTOM   There are things in this Comedy of Pyramus
and Thisby that will never please. First,   10
Pyramus must draw a Sword, to kill himself; which
the Ladies cannot abide. How answer you that?

SNOUT   Berlakin, a parlous Fear.

STARVELING   I believe, we must leave the killing,
out, when all is done.   15

BOTTOM   Not a whit: I have a Devise to make all well.
Write me a Prologue, and let the Prologue seem
to say, we will do no harm with our Swords, and
that Pyramus is not kill'd indeed; and for the
more better assurance, tell them that I   20
Pyramus am not Pyramus, but Bottom the Weaver.
This will put them out of fear.

QUINCE   Well: we will have such a Prologue, and it
shall be written in eight and six.

BOTTOM   No, make it two more; let it be written in   25
eight and eight.

29–30 **your self**   Normal grammar would call for *your selves* here. It is
characteristic of Bottom to 'call them generally' (I.ii.2).

32   **wild Foul**   The Quarto spelling for *Fowl* provides an amusing
comment on Bottom's solecism.

39   **defect**   Bottom means 'effect', but in fact the audience would
see the device Bottom proposes in this passage as a defect in
dramatic art. In a larger dramatic scheme, however, the one
that makes this a 'Sweet Comedy' (IV.ii.45), 'this Effect
Defective comes by Cause' (*Hamlet*, II.ii.103).

43   **it were pity of my Life**   My life would be in danger.

55   **Yes ... Night**   The always-prepared Peter Quince (see
I.ii.106–8) has brought a calendar to the rehearsal.

57   **Great Chamber Window**   the large window in the state room of
Theseus' palace.

59–60 **Bush of Thorns**   The Man in the Moon was thought by
peasants to carry a bundle of sticks and to be accompanied by
a dog. According to one legend, he had stolen them or picked
them up on the Sabbath. For that crime he had been banished
to the Moon, along with the dog who accompanied him.

61   **disfigure**   Quince means 'figure' or represent; but 'disfigure' is
precisely what Moonshine does. Compare Theseus' use of the
word 'disfigure' in I.i.51, and see the note to II.ii.104.

SNOUT   Will not the Ladies be afeard of the Lion?
STARVELING   I fear it, I promise you.
BOTTOM   Masters, you ought to consider with your
    self, to bring in (God shield us) a Lion among   30
    Ladies, is a most dreadful thing. For there is
    not a more fearful wild Foul than your Lion
    living; and we ought to look to't.
SNOUT   Therefore, another Prologue must tell, he is
    not a Lion.   35
BOTTOM   Nay, you must name his Name, and half his
    Face must be seen through the Lion's Neck, and
    he himself must speak through, saying thus, or
    to the same defect: 'Ladies,' or 'Fair Ladies,
    I would wish you,' or 'I would request you,' or   40
    'I would entreat you, not to fear, not to
    tremble; my Life for yours. If you think I come
    hither as a Lion, it were pity of my Life. No,
    I am no such thing: I am a Man as other Men
    are.' And there indeed, let him name his Name,   45
    and tell them plainly he is Snug, the Joiner.
QUINCE   Well: it shall be so. But there is two hard
    things: that is, to bring the Moon-light into a
    Chamber; for you know, Pyramus and Thisby meet
    by Moon-light.   50
SNOUT   Doth the Moon shine, that Night, we play our
    Play?
BOTTOM   A Calendar, a Calendar. Look in the
    Almanac; find out Moonshine, find out Moonshine.
QUINCE   Yes: it doth shine that Night.   55
BOTTOM   Why then, may you leave a Casement of the
    Great Chamber Window (where we play) open; and
    the Moon may shine in at the Casement.
QUINCE   Ay; or else one must come in, with a Bush of
    Thorns, and a Lantern, and say he comes to   60
    disfigure, or to present, the Person of
    Moonshine. Then, there is another thing: we must

65   **Chink**   small crack. In *Romeo and Juliet*, I.iv.232–33, just after the first meeting of Verona's equivalents to Ovid's Pyramus and Thisbe, the Nurse confides to Romeo that the man who 'can lay hold' of rich Capulet's daughter Juliet 'Shall have the Chinks'. The 'Story' Quince refers to in line 64 would have been familiar to Shakespeare's audience through Arthur Golding's translation (1565, 1567) of Ovid's *Metamorphoses*.

70   **Rough-cast**   a lime and gravel plaster to coat walls.

71   **thus**   Producers of the play have come up with a variety of amusing ways to interpret this crucial instruction about how to 'present Wall' (line 68).

78   **hempen Homespuns**   Puck (now labelled 'Robin' again) refers to the rustics by their apparel: garments crudely woven from a coarse fibre known as hemp.

79   **Cradle**   a term for her bower that reminds us of Titania's diminutive stature.

80   **toward**   forthcoming, in the offing.

83   PYRAMUS   The Quarto speech heading, reproduced here, suggests that Bottom has now *become* Pyramus. Soon he will undergo a second dramatic transformation. Meanwhile Flute has changed himself into Thisby.

83–84 **Flowers . . . Odours**   Quince insists on retaining the word meaning 'smelly' (*odorous*) over the word meaning 'hateful' (*odious*). Despite Quince's prompting, Bottom still gets the line wrong, saying 'odours' rather than 'odorous'. *Odorous* recalls II.i.110. *Savours* (both fragrances and flavours) recalls II.i.13.

88   PUCK   This speech heading, from the First Folio, alters what appears to have been an incorrect assignment of the speech to Quince in the Quarto.

91   **see a Noise**   one of many instances in the speech of the rustics where a verb relating to one sense is used with a noun relating to another. Bottom does this almost invariably.

have a Wall in the Great Chamber; for Pyramus
and Thisby, says the Story, did talk through
the Chink of a Wall.   65
SNOUT   You can never bring in a Wall. What say you,
Bottom?
BOTTOM   Some Man or other must present Wall. And
let him have some Plaster, or some Loam, or some
Rough-cast about him, to signify Wall. Or let   70
him hold his Fingers thus; and through that
Cranny, shall Pyramus and Thisby whisper.
QUINCE   If that may be, then all is well. Come, sit
down, every Mother's Son, and rehearse your
Parts. Pyramus, you begin. When you have   75
spoken your Speech, enter into that Brake, and
so every one according to his Cue.

Enter Robin.

ROBIN   What hempen Homespuns have we swagg'ring
here,
So near the Cradle of the Fairy Queen?
What, a Play toward? I'll be an Auditor,   80
An Actor too, perhaps, if I see cause.
QUINCE   Speak, Pyramus; Thisby, stand forth.
PYRAMUS   Thisby, the Flowers of odious Savours sweet.
QUINCE   Odours, 'odorous'.
PYRAMUS   Odours Savours sweet.
So hath thy Breath, my dearest Thisby dear.   85
But hark, a Voice: stay thou but here a while,
And by and by I will to thee appear.   *Exit.*
PUCK   A stranger Pyramus than e'er played here.
THISBY   Must I speak now?
QUINCE   Ay marry must you. For you must understand,   90
he goes but to see a Noise, that he heard, and is
to come again.
THISBY   Most radiant Pyramus, most lily-white of Hue,

64

95   **brisky Juvenal**   lusty juvenile or youth.
      eke . . . Jew   an abbreviated repetition of *Juvenal*, in all
         likelihood. The early texts use a spelling that calls to mind a
         famous Roman satirist. Compare *Love's Labour's Lost*,
         III.i.69, where Shakespeare enjoys a similar jest at Armado's
         expense. *Eke* is an archaic form for 'also'.

98   **Ninus**   the legendary founder of Nineveh; Pyramus and Thisbe
         rendezvous at his tomb in the version of the story told in
         Book IV of Ovid's *Metamorphoses*. Quince succeeds only
         temporarily in correcting the pronunciation of the King's
         name: Bottom again refers to 'Ninny's Tomb' when the play
         is performed in Act V. *Ninny* meant a silly fool.

S.D. **Enter . . . Ass-head**   The Folio stage-direction, reproduced here,
         indicates that 'Pyramus' now has an apt addition to his
         original costume: an ass's head to supplant his own.

104   **'If I were fair, Thisby . . .'**   To make sense in terms of the
         playlet (as distinguished from the play that incorporates it),
         the comma should precede rather than follow 'fair'. The First
         Quarto and First Folio texts place the comma so that 'fair'
         applies to Bottom rather than to Thisby. In view of Bottom's
         'monstrous' appearance at this moment, that ironic touch
         enhances the humour.

105   **haunted**   victims of supernatural charms. Quince's verb recalls
         II.ii.91.

107   **Round**   a round dance. Compare II.i.140–41.

113– **a Knavery of them**   a practical joke of theirs.
14

117– **Asshead of your own**   Bottom's reply suggests that Snout
18   gestures in such a way as to mimic Bottom's ass ears.

Of Colour like the red Rose, on triumphant
Brier;
Most brisky Juvenal, and eke most lovely Jew;   95
As true as truest Horse, that yet would never
tyre.
I'll meet thee, Pyramus, at Ninny's Tomb.

QUINCE   'Ninus' Tomb', man. Why, you must not speak
that yet. That you answer to Pyramus. You speak
all your Part at once, Cues and all. – Pyramus,   100
enter. Your Cue is past: it is 'never tire'.

THISBY   O, as true as truest Horse, that yet would never
tire.

Enter Pyramus with the Ass-head.

PYRAMUS   If I were fair, Thisby, I were onely thine.
QUINCE   O monstrous! O strange! We are haunted.   105
Pray, Masters. Fly, Masters. Help.
                                    The Clowns all exit.
ROBIN   I'll follow you: I'll lead you about a Round,
Through Bog, through Bush, through Brake,
through Brier;
Sometime a Horse I'll be, sometime a Hound,
A Hog, a headless Bear, sometime a Fire;   110
And neigh, and bark, and grunt, and roar,
and burn,
Like Horse, Hound, Hog, Bear, Fire, at
every turn.   *Exit.*
BOTTOM   Why do they run away? This is a Knavery
of them to make me afeard.

Enter Snout.

SNOUT   O Bottom, thou art chaung'd. What do I   115
see on thee?
BOTTOM   What do you see? You see an Ass-head
of your own. Do you?   [*Exit Snout.*]

120 **translated**   transformed. It is fitting that a comic
metamorphosis should occur in this play, which draws so
heavily on Ovid's *Metamorphoses*. Compare I.i.191.

126 **Woosel**   ousel or blackbird. The 'Lullaby' that will awaken
Titania features birds of a much more 'common Rate' (line
155) than the nightingale chorus to which she drifted into
sleep in II.ii.9–30.

128 **Throstle**   thrush.

132– **Cuckow ... Cuckow, never so**   The resemblance between the
37   sound 'cuckow' (here rendered as it is spelled in the early
texts) and the word 'cuckold' (the name for a husband whose
wife has been unfaithful to him) makes a man 'mark' (heed)
and dread the cuckoo's 'Note' (song). He hopes its message is
not applicable to himself, but he is afraid to say for certain
that it is not. Since it is difficult to determine just what is
being quoted directly here, this edition reproduces the line as
it appears in the Quarto.

135 **set his Wit to**   try to match wits with. Like *Will*, *Wit* could refer
to the genitalia of either gender (see *As You Like It*,
IV.i.168–87).

140 **enthralled**   This word recalls I.i.136.

147 **make them Friends**   use their good offices to reconcile them.

148 **gleek**   jest. Bottom is pleased with the witticism he has just
offered about reason and love.

150– **if ... turn**   Bottom is saying: if I could figure out how to get
52   out of these woods, I could take care of myself. The phrase
'serve mine own turn' is frequently erotic in implication (see
Titus Andronicus, II.i.95–96). This is fitting, because a sexual
infatuation with a beast is precisely what Oberon wants to
inflict upon his Queen. See II.i.176–85.

Enter Quince.

QUINCE   Bless thee, Bottom, bless thee. Thou art
    translated.   *Exit.*   120
BOTTOM   I see their Knavery: this is to make an Ass
    of me, to fright me, if they could. But I will
    not stir from this place, do what they can. I
    will walk up and down here, and I will sing,
    that they shall hear I am not afraid.   125
        The Woosel Cock, so black of hue,
            With orange-tawny Bill;
        The Throstle, with his Note so true,
            The Wren, with little Quill –
TITANIA   What Angel wakes me from my flow'ry Bed?   130
BOTTOM   The Finch, the Sparrow, and the Lark;
        The plainsong Cuckow grey,
        Whose Note full many a Man doth mark
            And dares not answer nay.
    For indeed, who would set his Wit to so   135
    Foolish a Bird? Who would give a Bird
    The Lie, though he cry Cuckow, never so.
TITANIA   I pray thee, gentle Mortal, sing again;
    Mine Ear is much enamour'd of thy Note.
    So is mine Eye enthralled to thy Shape;   140
    And thy fair Virtue's Force perforce doth move
        me
    On the first View to say, to swear, I love thee.
BOTTOM   Me thinks, Mistress, you should have little
    Reason for that. And yet, to say the truth,
    Reason and Love keep little Company together   145
    nowadays. The more the pity that some honest
    Neighbours will not make them Friends. Nay, I
    can gleek, upon occasion.
TITANIA   Thou art as Wise as thou art Beautiful.
BOTTOM   Not so, neither; but if I had Wit enough to   150
    get out of this Wood, I have enough to serve
    mine own turn.

154 **whether** pronounced with the value of a one-syllable word.

155 **Rate** rank, degree.

156 **(The Summer . . . State)** Titania says that the Summer 'still' (always) pays homage to and serves her 'State' (her royal presence). One indication of Titania's 'State' throughout this scene is the fact that she speaks verse while Bottom continues to speak prose.

161– **And I . . . go** Titania says that she will purify ('purge') Bottom
62 of his corporeality (his 'Mortal Grossness' or human flesh) so that he will be able to move about in Fairyland as a weightless 'Airy Spirit' like herself. *Mortal* recalls I.i.101, 135.

163 **Moth** This name could signify either 'moth' or 'mote' (for which *moth* was a common spelling). See the note to V.i.321.

164– **PEASEBLOSSOM . . . go?** In the Quarto and Folio the five lines
68 presented here (and in all modern editions) constitute a single line with the speech heading '*Fairies*'.

170 **gambol** skip and jump.

171 **Apricocks** original spelling of *apricots*.
Dewberries blackberries.

173 **Humble-bees** bumblebees; called *humblebees* because of their loud humming sound.

174 **Night-tapers** candles.
waxen Thighs thighs coated with beeswax.

175 **Glow-worm's** In the early printings there are seldom clear distinctions among simple plurals, singular possessives, and plural possessives. Here, for example, the Quarto's *glow-wormes* could just as logically be rendered *Glow-worms'*.

179 **Courtesies** both (a) deferential service, and (b) curtsies (as signalled by 'Nod to him').

183 **cry . . . mercy** beseech your worships to pardon me. The Quarto's *worships* (a term of respect) could just as easily be interpreted to mean *Worships'* or *Worship's*.

TITANIA   Out of this Wood do not desire to go;
Thou shalt remain here, whether thou wilt or no.
I am a Spirit of no common Rate   155
(The Summer still doth tend upon my State),
And I do love thee: therefore go with me.
I'll give thee Fairies to attend on thee,
And they shall fetch thee Jewels from the Deep,
And sing, while thou on pressed Flowers dost
    sleep.   160
And I will purge thy Mortal Grossness so
That thou shalt like an Airy Spirit go.
Peaseblossom, Cobweb, Moth, and Mustardseed?

Enter four Fairies.

PEASEBLOSSOM   Ready.
COBWEB   And I.   165
MOTH   And I.
MUSTARDSEED   And I.
ALL   Where shall we go?
TITANIA   Be kind and courteous to this Gentleman:
Hop in his Walks, and gambol in his Eyes;   170
Feed him with Apricocks and Dewberries,
With purple Grapes, green Figs, and Mulberries;
The Honeybags steal from the Humble-bees,
And for Night-tapers crop their waxen Thighs
And light them at the fiery Glow-worm's Eyes,   175
To have my Love to Bed, and to arise;
And pluck the Wings from painted Butterflies
To fan the Moon-beams from his sleeping Eyes;
Nod to him, Elves, and do him Courtesies.
1 FAIRY   Hail, Mortal, hail.   180
2 FAIRY   Hail.
3 FAIRY   Hail.
BOTTOM   I cry your Worships mercy heartily. — I
beseech your Worship's Name?

185 **desire . . . acquaintance**   wish to know you better as we become more acquainted.

188 **make bold with you**   presume to call for your services.
Cobwebs were used to stop the flow of blood.

189 **Peaseblossom**   pea blossom.

190 **commend me**   convey my respects.
Squash   an unripe peapod.

191 **Peascod**   a ripe peapod.

196 **Patience**   forbearance in suffering injuries. Mustard is a condiment frequently used to season beef, and one that can make the eater's 'Eyes water'. But Bottom's reference to Mustardseed's 'Patience' may also relate to the Parable of the Mustard Seed, comparing the meekness and patience required for 'the Kingdom of God' to 'a grain of mustard seed, which, when it is sown in the earth, is less than all the seeds that be in the earth', but 'it groweth up, and becometh greater than all herbs' (Mark 4:30–32).

199– **Eyes water**   from mustard's spiciness, but here tactfully
200 described as if the cause were grief.

202 **Bower**   den secluded by overhanging boughs.

205 **enforced Chastity**   instance of chastity violated (in this case, Bottom's). Titania has no intention of having the Moon impose any 'enforced Chastity' on her. She will 'tie up' her 'Lover's Tongue' to impose her will upon him. *Wat'ry Eye* (line 203) echoes lines 199–200 and recalls I.i.120 and II.i.162. In the process it reminds us of Hermia's situation, and of the 'enforced Chastity' (see I.i.65–78) she has fled Athens to evade.

COBWEB   Cobweb.   185
BOTTOM   I shall desire you of more acquaintance,
    good Master Cobweb. If I cut my Finger, I shall
    make bold with you. – Your Name, honest Gentleman?
PEASEBLOSSOM   Peaseblossom.
BOTTOM   I pray you commend me to Mistress Squash,   190
    your Mother, and to Master Peascod, your Father.
    Good Master Peaseblossom, I shall desire you
    of more acquaintance too. – Your Name, I beseech
    you, Sir?
MUSTARDSEED   Mustardseed.   195
BOTTOM   Good Master Mustardseed, I know your
    Patience well. That same cowardly, giantlike Ox-beef
    hath devour'd many a Gentleman of your House. I
    promise you, your Kindred hath made my Eyes
    water ere now. I desire you more acquaintance,   200
    good Master Mustardseed.
TITANIA   Come wait upon him; lead him to my Bower.
    The Moon, me thinks, looks with a wat'ry Eye;
    And when she weeps, weeps every little Flower,
        Lamenting some enforced Chastity.   205
    Tie up my Lover's Tongue; bring him silently.

Exeunt.

III.ii   This scene takes place at a nearby point in the wood.

3   **in extremity**   to an extreme, excessively. *Dote* recalls II.i.171.

5   **Night-rule**   It is because of Puck's 'Night-rule' (nocturnal activities) that Oberon calls the grove 'haunted'. *Haunted* recalls II.i.105.

6–7   **My . . . Bower**   In these two lines this edition adheres to the punctuation in the Quarto. Most editors place a full stop after line 6 and a comma after line 7. *Monster* recalls II.ii.103; it's a word that derives from the Latin *monstrare*, 'to show or to warn', and in this play manifestations of the monstrous tend eventually to prompt recognitions and revelations.

7   **close and consecrated**   enclosed and set apart.

8   **Dull**   drowsy.

9   **Patches**   fools, so called because of their motley apparel.
    rude Mechanicals   crude craftsmen. *Rude* recalls II.i.152 and anticipates line 262.

13   **shallowest Thickskin**   Puck contrasts Bottom's shallow wit with his thick (coarse and calloused) skin.
    barrain   barren, empty of intellect or learning. Compare I.i.72, and see the note to I.i.70.
    Sort   group, company.

15   **Brake**   thicket (see III.i.3–6, 75–77).

17   **Nole**   noodle, top of the head (called a 'Scalp' in IV.i.67).

18   **Anon**   shortly thereafter.

19   **my Mimic**   my actor; that is, Bottom.

20   **creeping Fouler**   both (a) fowler, stealthy bird hunter, and (b) fouler (despoiler, foiler).

21   **russet-pated Choughs**   rusty-headed jackdaws; *Choughs* is pronounced 'chuffs'. Most of Shakespeare's references to choughs are derisive. See, for example, *Hamlet*, V.ii.87–88, where the Prince refers to a foolish young courtier as 'a Chough, but, as I say, spacious in the Possession of Dirt', and *The Tempest*, II.i.247–48, where Antonio, referring to Gonzalo, tells Sebastian 'I my self could make / A Chough of as deep Chat'.
    many in sort   many in one group.

Scene 2

Enter King of Fairies.

OBERON   I wonder if Titania be awak'd;
  Then what it was that next came in her Eye,
  Which she must dote on in extremity.

Enter Robin Goodfellow.

  Here comes my Messenger. – How now, mad Spirit?
  What Night-rule now about this haunted
    Grove?   5
PUCK   My Mistress with a Monster is in love,
  Near to her close and consecrated Bower.
  While she was in her Dull and Sleeping Hour,
  A crew of Patches, rude Mechanicals,
  That work for Bread upon Athenian Stalls,   10
  Were met together to rehearse a Play
  Intended for great Theseus' Nuptial Day.
  The shallowest Thickskin of that barrain Sort,
  Who Pyramus presented in their Sport,
  Forsook his Scene and ent'red in a Brake,   15
  When I did him at this advantage take:
  An Ass's Nole I fixed on his Head.
  Anon his Thisby must be answered,
  And forth my Mimic comes. When they him spy,
  As wild Geese that the creeping Fouler eye,   20
  Or russet-pated Choughs, many in sort,
  Rising and cawing at the Gun's Report,
  Sever themselves and madly sweep the Sky,
  So at his Sight away his Fellows fly.

25   **at our Stamp**   Puck's use of the plural 'our' is probably
      intended as a reminder of the various creatures he pretended
      to be (see III.i.107–12) as he stamped about the wood putting
      the rustics to rout.

27   **Sense**   both (a) common sense, and (b) senses. Compare II.ii.51.

30   **yielders**   those who yield; that is, the frightened rustics. *Catch*
      (can be snatched) recalls I.i.186–89.

31   **distracted**   frantic, frenzied. Compare *wodde* (II.i.192).

32   **translated**   transformed. Compare III.i.120.

35   **devise**   scheme, plan. This verb recalls III.i.16.

36   **latch'd**   snared, trapped.

38   **took**   charmed, cast under a spell.

40   **of force**   of necessity. Compare II.i.26, III.i.202–6.

44   **Lay Breath . . . Foe**   Save words so bitter for your bitter enemy.

45   **chide**   rebuke, scold. Compare II.i.145.

48   **Being o'er shoes in Blood**   since you have already shed enough
      blood to create a pool above the tops of your shoes.
      Shakespeare uses similar imagery in *The Two Gentlemen* of
      Verona, I.i.24–27. And there is a variation on it in *Macbeth*,
      III.iv.134–36.

53–55 **This whole Earth . . . Antipodes**   Hermia imagines a hole big
      enough for the Moon to pass ('creep') through and thereby
      disturb or eclipse ('displease') the Sun's ('Her Brother's')
      midday tide in the Antipodes (the Southern Hemisphere and,
      from the position of Britain, specifically the area centred
      around Australia, still referred to as 'Down Under'). The
      literal meaning of *Antipodes* is 'with the feet opposite'; it
      refers to those who live on the far side of the globe.

And at our Stamp here o'er and o'er one falls,   25
He 'Murther' cries, and help from Athens calls.
Their Sense thus weak, lost with their Fears
   thus strong,
Made Senseless Things begin to do them wrong:
For Briers and Thorns at their Apparel snatch;
Some Sleeves, some Hats; from yielders all
   things catch.   30
I led them on, in this distracted Fear,
And left sweet Pyramus translated there.
When in that moment (so it came to pass)
Titania wak'd, and straightway lov'd an Ass.
OBERON   This falls out better than I could devise.   35
  But hast thou yet latch'd the Athenian's Eyes
  With the Love-juice as I did bid thee do?
ROBIN   I took him sleeping (that is finish'd too)
  And the Athenian Woman by his side,
  That when he wak'd of force she must be ey'd.   40

Enter Demetrius and Hermia.

OBERON   Stand close: this is the same Athenian.
ROBIN   This is the Woman, but not this the Man.
DEMETRIUS   O, why rebuke you him that loves you so?
  Lay Breath so bitter on your bitter Foe.
HERMIA   Now I but chide, but I should use thee
   worse: 45
  For thou, I fear, hast given me cause to curse.
  If thou hast slain Lysander in his sleep,
  Being o'er shoes in Blood, plunge in the deep
  And kill me too.
  The Sun was not so true unto the Day   50
  As he to me. Would he have stolen away
  From sleeping Hermia? I'll believe as soon
  This whole Earth may be bor'd, and that the Moon
  May through the Centre creep, and so displease

61 **yonder Venus** Demetrius refers to the planet Venus 'in her
glimmering Sphere', but he is also thinking about the Goddess
of Love. As he talks to Hermia, he feels Venus' influence; but
because of Hermia's 'stern Cruelty' (her refusal to entertain
this courtly lover's suit), Venus still seems remote ('yonder').
Glimmering recalls II.i.77 and anticipates V.i.395. Lines
60–61 recall the imagery of III.i.110–11.

69 **look'd** This word is stressed in a way that conveys the meaning
'even look'd'.

71 **a Worm, an Adder** both are words for snake or serpent.

72 **doubler Tongue** referring both to the serpent's forked tongue
and to the duplicity associated with it through the story of
Man's fall from innocence in the Garden of Eden. Compare
II.ii.9.

74 **mispris'd Mood** mistaken fit of anger. To 'misprize' is to take
wrongly, literally to value at the wrong price. Compare line
90.

76 **for ought that I can tell** from anything I can observe.

78 **therefore** therefor; for it.

80 **part I** Editors normally add *so* after this phrase. Doing so
avoids a break in a series of rhyming couplets; but a dramatic
departure from the expected norm would reinforce the breach
Hermia depicts, and may well have been precisely what the
playwright devised here. See the notes to I.i.219, I.ii.31 and
69, and III.i.39 for discussions of similar 'defects' elsewhere in
the play.

82 **Vein** mood, disposition. Here as in I.ii.41, *Vein* is spelled *vaine*
in the Quarto.

84–87 **So Sorrow's Heaviness ... Stay** Sorrow and sleep are
personified as participants in a business transaction. Sleep has
borrowed from Sorrow almost to the point of becoming
'Bankrout' (bankrupt). But Sleep will now pay back some of
its debt to Sorrow if for Sleep's 'Tender' (offer) Demetrius will
'make some stay' (pause long enough to accept payment). In
other words, because of Demetrius' pining for Hermia, he has
gone too long without sleep and is now preparing to lie down
and rest. *Stay* recalls II.ii.90.

Her Brother's Noontide with th' Antipodes.   55
It cannot be but thou hast murd'red him.
So should a Murth'rer look: so dead, so grim.
DEMETRIUS   So should the Murth'red look, and so
   should I,
Pierc'd through the Heart with your stern
   Cruelty.
Yet you, the Murth'rer, look as bright, as clear,   60
As yonder Venus in her glimmering Sphere.
HERMIA   What's this to my Lysander? Where is he?
Ah good Demetrius, wilt thou give him me?
DEMETRIUS   I had rather give his Carcass to my Hounds.
HERMIA   Out, Dog; out, Cur. Thou driv'st me past the
   bounds   65
Of Maiden's Patience. Hast thou slain him then?
Henceforth be never numb'red among Men.
O once tell true; tell true even for my sake:
Durst thou have look'd upon him being awake?
And hast thou kill'd him sleeping? O brave touch!   70
Could not a Worm, an Adder, do so much?
An Adder did it: for with doubler Tongue
Than thine, thou Serpent, never Adder stung.
DEMETRIUS   You spend your Passion on a mispris'd
   Mood:
I am not guilty of Lysander's Blood,   75
Nor is he dead for ought that I can tell.
HERMIA   I pray thee tell me then that he is well.
DEMETRIUS   And if I could, what should I get
   therefore?
HERMIA   A privilege never to see me more.
And from thy hated presence part I: 80
See me no more, whether he be dead or no.   *Exit.*
DEMETRIUS   There is no following her in this Fierce
   Vein;
Here therefore for a while I will remain.
So Sorrow's Heaviness doth heavier grow

88   **mistaken**   both (a) erred, and (b) mis-taken (see the note to line 38).

90   **Misprision**   misapprehension, mistake. The word derives from misprize. Compare line 74.

91   **turn'd**   changed, metamorphosed. This verb recalls III.i.50–52. For a look at the more serious implications *turn* can carry, see *Othello*, IV.i.254–58.

93   **confounding Oath on Oath**   making and breaking one vow on top of another. Compare I.i.168–78, and see *The Merchant of Venice*, V.i.1–22.

96   **Fancy-sick**   love-sick. Compare II.i.161–65.
        pale of Cheer   pale of cheek. *Cheer* recalls I.i.122, 128–31.

97   **Sighs of Love . . . dear**   Helena's sighs have depleted her blood supply. It was proverbial that every sigh or tear of sorrow caused the loss of a drop of blood. *Blood* recalls I.i.68, 135.

99   **against she do appear**   in preparation for her appearance. Compare the use of *against* in I.i.125.

101   **Tartar's Bow**   The bows of the Tartars (warriors from Asia Minor) were extraordinarily powerful. *Bow* recalls I.ii.113 and II.i.159.

105   **espy**   see. As he speaks lines 102–9 Oberon anoints Demetrius' eyes with a dose of the same potion he and Puck have deployed earlier for Titania (II.ii.33–40) and Lysander (II.ii.84–88).

108   **by**   nearby.

For Debt that Bankrout Sleep doth Sorrow owe,   85
Which now in some slight measure it will pay
If for his Tender here I make some Stay.
                                        Lie down.
OBERON   What hast thou done? Thou hast mistaken
   quite,
And laid the Love-juice on some True-love's
   Sight.
Of thy Misprision must perforce ensue   90
Some True-love turn'd and not a False turn'd
   True.
ROBIN   Then Fate o'errules, that One Man holding
   Troth,
A Million fail, confounding Oath on Oath.
OBERON   About the Wood, go swifter than the Wind,
And Helena of Athens look thou find.   95
All Fancy-sick she is and pale of Cheer,
With Sighs of Love, that costs the fresh Blood
   dear.
By some Illusion see thou bring her here;
I'll charm his Eyes against she do appear.
ROBIN   I go, I go, look how I go: 100
Swifter than Arrow from the Tartar's Bow.   *Exit.*
OBERON   Flower of this Purple Dye,
         Hit with Cupid's Archery,
         Sink in Apple of his Eye;
         When his Love he doth espy,   105
         Let her shine as gloriously
         As the Venus of the Sky.
         When thou wak'st, if she be by,
         Beg of her for Remedy.

                  Enter Puck.

PUCK   Captain of our Fairy Band,   110
⌐⎯⎯   Helena is here at hand;

113 **Fee** recompense.

114 **fond Pageant** display of love's folly. *Fond* recalls II.ii.94.

119 **Sport** amusement. Compare line 14, where it refers to a
   theatrical entertainment.
   alone all by itself. Frequently, *alone* puns on 'all one', and
   there is a hint of such wordplay here.

121 **befall** come to pass.
   prepost'rously ludicrously. The literal meaning of *preposterous*
   is 'with the rear (Latin *posterus*) in the front (*prae-*) position',
   a notion conveyed in the expression 'with the cart before the
   horse'. The preposterous is, of course, the essence of comedy.

122 **woo in Scorn** pretend to woo you while really scorning you.

124 **Look when I vow** whenever I vow.

124– **Vows . . . appears** Vows born of tears (or carried by tears) are
25   proven by their origin ('Nativity') to be true. *Borne* can mean
   either (a) borne, or (b) born.

127 **badge of Faith** Lysander is referring to his tears, which he
   depicts as the insignia of fidelity.

128 **advance your Cunning** increase (and press forward) your
   deceitfulness.

129 **Truth kills Truth . . . Fray** Helena means that if Lysander is
   telling the truth now, he 'kills' the truth (troth) he swore to
   Hermia earlier. The result is a 'Fray' (conflict) that results in a
   'divelish holy' self-contradiction.

131– **Weigh Oath . . . Tales** Helena says that if Lysander balances
33   his two oaths on 'two Scales', they will cancel each other and
   'Nothing weigh'.

134 **Tales** lies. Helena may be punning on 'Tails', the lightest
   portions of animal anatomies. See the note to II.i.54.

137 **perfect Divine** complete embodiment of divinity. Most editors
   follow the Folio and insert a comma after *perfect*. Compare
   line 227, where editors usually add a comma after *Precious*.
   Demetrius' arousal recalls the awakenings of Lysander in
   II.ii.109 and Titania in II.i.130.

139 **Crystal is muddy** Demetrius says that compared to Helena's
   eyes, even crystal (symbolizing a clarity so pure as to be
   completely transparent) is muddy.
   in Show in appearance, display.

And the Youth mistook by me
Pleading for a Lover's Fee.
Shall we their fond Pageant see?
Lord, what Fools these Mortals be!   115
OBERON   Stand aside: the Noise they make
Will cause Demetrius to awake.
PUCK   Then will Two at once woo One:
That must needs be Sport alone.
And those things do best please me   120
That befall prepost'rously.

Enter Lysander and Helena.

LYSANDER   Why should you think that I should woo in
Scorn?
Scorn and Derision never come in Tears.
Look when I vow I weep; and Vows so borne,
In their Nativity all Truth appears.   125
How can these things in me seem Scorn to you?
Bearing the badge of Faith to prove them True.
HELENA   You do advance your Cunning more and more;
When Truth kills Truth, O divelish holy Fray!
These Vows are Hermia's: will you give her o'er?   130
Weigh Oath with Oath, and you will Nothing weigh:
Your Vows to her and me, put in two Scales,
Will even weigh, and both as light as Tales.
LYSANDER   I had no Judgement when to her I swore.
HELENA   Nor none, in my Mind, now you give her o'er.   135
LYSANDER   Demetrius loves her, and he loves not you.
DEMETRIUS   O Helen, Goddess, Nymph, perfect Divine,
To what, my Love, shall I compare thine Eyne!
Crystal is muddy. O how ripe in Show

82

141 **Taurus** a mountain range in Turkey.

142 **turns to a Crow** turns black in comparison.

144 **Bliss** blessedness, the state of those in Heaven. *Seal* recalls
    I.i.84.

145 **Spight** spite, malice. So also in line 194.

148 **Injury** injustice (from *juris*, 'justice'), harm.

152 **use** treat. So also in line 45. Compare II.i.205, 210.

153 **superpraise** overpraise.
    Parts both bodily parts and qualities, attributes. Compare
    V.i.28 for a more comical reference to a part.

157 **trim** brave, worthy.

158 **conjure** summon, as a magician calls up evil spirits.

159 **Sort** kind.

160 **extort** torture; literally, 'twist out'. *Patience* recalls II.i.196.

164 **hear** Most editors emend the Quarto's *heare* to *here*; but *hear*
    makes equally good sense. To an audience of course, it would
    be difficult if not impossible to tell the difference. The Folio
    prints *here*.

170 **ere** both (a) before, and (b) ever.

171 **as Guest-wise sojourn'd** visited as a guest.

Thy Lips, those kissing Cherries, tempting grow!   140
That pure congealed White, high Taurus' Snow,
Fand with the Eastern Wind, turns to a Crow
When thou holdst up thy Hand. O let me kiss
This Princess of pure White, this Seal of Bliss.
HELENA   O Spight! O Hell! I see you all are bent   145
To set against me for your Merriment.
If you were Civil and knew Courtesy,
You would not do me thus much Injury.
Can you not hate me, as I know you do,
But you must join in Souls to mock me too?   150
If you were Men, as Men you are in Show,
You would not use a gentle Lady so:
To vow and swear and superpraise my Parts,
When I am sure you hate me with your Hearts.
You both are Rivals and love Hermia.   155
And now both Rivals to mock Helena.
A trim Exploit, a manly Enterprise,
To conjure Tears up in a poor Maid's Eyes
With your Derision. None of Noble Sort
Would so offend a Virgin, and extort   160
A poor Soul's Patience, all to make you Sport.
LYSANDER   You are unkind, Demetrius; be not so,
For you love Hermia; this you know I know.
And hear with all Good Will, with all my Heart,
In Hermia's Love I yield you up my Part.   165
And yours of Helena to me bequeath,
Whom I do love, and will do till my Death.
HELENA   Never did Mockers waste more idle Breath.
DEMETRIUS   Lysander, keep thy Hermia: I will none.
If ere I lov'd her, all that Love is gone.   170
My Heart to her but as Guest-wise sojourn'd;
And now to Helen is it Home return'd,
There to remain.
LYSANDER   Helen, it is not so.

175   **Least** lest. *Least* is the normal Shakespearean spelling for a word whose original meaning was 'by the less that'; at times it plays on the more usual meaning of *least*. Compare line 385.
        aby buy, pay for; the word is accented on the second syllable.

176   **thy Love . . . thy Dear** The context calls for stress on these phrases in the line in order to register its emotional force: 'Loók whère / thý Lové / còmes: yón / dĕr ĭs / thý Déar'.

177   **his** its. The usual forms of the neuter singular possessive in Shakespeare are *his* and *it*.

177–   **Dark Night . . . Recompense** Hermia says that by impairing
80   sight, night strengthens the sense of hearing. *Quick* means both (a) alert, and (b) rapid. Compare I.i.149. *Recompense* recalls *Fee* (line 113) and the imagery of indebtedness in lines 83–87.

182   **unkindly** both (a) cruelly, unfeelingly, and (b) uncharacteristically (unlike your kind of person).

184   **press** urge, compel. Compare II.ii.71. *Stay* recalls II.ii.90.

186   **bide** remain.

187   **engilds** makes golden.

188   **Oes and Eyes** 'Oes' were circular spangles used as ornaments on fancy garments. Lysander also puns on the plurals of the vowels *o* and *i*.

190   **bare** bore. Again, though, a theatre audience could understand Lysander to be saying *bear* (compare *hear* in line 164).

192   **Confederacy** alliance, conspiracy.

194   **in spight of me** in contempt of me, to spite me.

195   **Injurious** unjust. Compare lines 148, 219.

197   **bait** goad, torment. Derived from 'bite', the word refers to popular sports in which dogs were set upon bears or bulls tied to stakes. Helena, seemingly besieged by her friends, feels like the victim of such 'false Sport' (line 194, echoing line 119).

DEMETRIUS   Disparage not the Faith thou dost not
   know,
   Least to thy Peril thou aby it dear.   175
   Look where thy Love comes: yonder is thy Dear.

Enter Hermia.

HERMIA   Dark Night, that from the Eye his Function
   takes,
   The Ear more quick of Apprehension makes.
   Wherein it doth impair the Seeing Sense,
   It pays the Hearing double Recompense.   180
   Thou art not by mine Eye, Lysander, found:
   Mine Ear, I thank it, brought me to thy Sound.
   But why unkindly didst thou leave me so?
LYSANDER   Why should he stay whom Love doth press
   to go?
HERMIA   What Love could press Lysander from my
   side?   185
LYSANDER   Lysander's Love, that would not let him
   bide:
   Fair Helena, who more engilds the Night
   Than all yon fiery Oes and Eyes of Light.
   Why seek'st thou me? Could not this make thee
   know
   The hate I bare thee made me leave thee so?   190
HERMIA   You speak not as you think: it cannot be.
HELENA   Lo: she is one of this Confederacy.
   Now I perceive they have conjoin'd all three
   To fashion this false Sport in spight of me.
   — Injurious Hermia, most ungrateful Maid,   195
   Have you conspir'd, have you with these
   contriv'd,
   To bait me with this foul Derision?
   Is all the Counsel that we two have shar'd,
   The Sisters' Vows, the Hours that we have spent,

200 **hasty-footed Time** Time is here personified; Helena recalls a
period when she and Hermia scolded it for parting them too
hastily. *Chid* (chided) recalls line 45.

203 **Artificial Gods** In the lines that follow, Helena attributes
quasi-divine powers to herself and Hermia. *Artificial* refers
here to artifice, the skill of an artist. Compare I.i.192–93 and
II.ii.110–11.

204 **Needles** pronounced in a gliding fashion, to yield a single
stressed syllable.

208 **incorporate** combined into a single body.

209 **Cherry** This image recalls line 140.
Parted divided into separate parts.

213 **Two ... Heraldry** It is consistent with the other powers
Helena credits to herself and Hermia that these dear friends
should also be able to bring to life, and combine in 'one Crest'
(line 214), two coats of arms. According to Helena, she and
Hermia combined to become the first living, breathing coats
of arms in the history of heraldry. Modern editions normally
emend the line to read 'Two of the first, like coats in
heraldry'. Compare II.ii.51–56.

214 **Due** owing, belonging. Compare I.i.37, 154.

215 **auncient** time-honoured.

217 **friendly** Here the word has the force of its original meaning:
'friend-like'.

220 **passionate** here pronounced as a two-syllable word (páshnate).
This word occurs only in the Folio. It fills out a line that is
metrically short in the Quarto, and it may have been added by
someone other than the playwright who could well have
wanted a dramatic interruption of metrical regularity here.
See the note to line 80.

227 **Precious Celestial** The Folio adds a comma here, and most
editors follow suit. Compare line 137.
Wherefore why; for what reason.

230 **forsooth** in truth, indeed; used here to intensify the strongly
stressed word *me*.

232 **in Grace** in favour.

When we have chid the hasty-footed Time   200
For parting us – O, is all forgot?
All Schooldays' Friendship, Childhood Innocence?
We, Hermia, like two Artificial Gods,
Have with our Needles created both one Flower,
Both on one Sampler, sitting on one Cushion,   205
Both warbling of one Song, both in one Key:
As if our Hands, our Sides, Voices, and Minds
Had been incorporate. So we grew together,
Like to a Double Cherry: seeming Parted,
But yet an Union in Partition,   210
Two lovely Berries moulded on one Stem.
So with two seeming Bodies but one Heart,
Two of the first Life-coats in Heraldry,
Due but to one, and crowned with one Crest.
And will you rent our auncient Love asunder   215
To join with Men in scorning your poor Friend?
It is not friendly, 'tis not maidenly.
Our Sex as well as I may chide you for it,
Though I alone do feel the Injury.
HERMIA   I am amazed at your passionate Words: 220
I scorn you not; it seems that you scorn me.
HELENA   Have you not set Lysander, as in Scorn,
To follow me, and praise my Eyes and Face?
And made your other Love, Demetrius
(Who even but now did spurn me with his Foot),   225
To call me Goddess, Nymph, Divine, and Rare,
Precious Celestial? Wherefore speaks he this
To her he hates? And wherefore doth Lysander
Deny your Love (so rich within his Soul)
And tender me, forsooth, Affection,   230
But by your setting on, by your Consent?
What though I be not so in Grace as you,
So hung upon with Love, so fortunate,
But miserable most, to love unlov'd?
This you should pity rather than despise.   235

237 **I do** Helena's brief sentence can be read two ways: (a) I do [understand], or (b) Ay, do [continue this sport at my expense].
Persever Keep it up! This old spelling of *persevere* retains the original stress on the second syllable.

238 **Make . . . me** mock me with facial gestures. *Jest* (line 239) is spelled *ieast* in the Quarto; see the note to II.i.44, and compare line 265.

240 **well carried** well executed. *Sport* echoes lines 119, 194.
shall be chronicled shall make history.

242 **You . . . Argument** You would not hold me up as an example, a subject for ridicule.

243 **Fault** flaw (literally, 'crack'), deficiency. Compare *crazed*, I.i.92. Helena now sees herself as faced with choices (line 244) that recall the ones offered Hermia in I.i.83–90.

245 **my Excuse** explanation for my behaviour (without any implication that it needs to be pardoned).

247 **scorn** mock, treat contemptuously. We should note that at this point Hermia and Demetrius both assume that Helena is correct and that Lysander is only feigning love for Helena. Hermia's line 247 and Demetrius' line 248 are both directed to Lysander.

250 **Praise** In both the First Quarto and First Folio, this word is spelled *praise*, but it could also represent *prays*, a coinage to pluralise the quoted word *pray* (synonymous with 'entreat', line 249). The actor playing Lysander could convey this sense with a prayer-like gesture. Modern editions normally emend *praise* to *prayers*. *Praise* echoes line 153.

257 **Ethiope** Another allusion to Hermia's dark complexion. Conventional definitions of beauty stressed 'fairness' as the ideal.

258 **Take on as** pretend.

259 **go** walk with me, come.

260 **Bur** a prickly seedcase, and by extension a person who sticks like a bur.

261 **Serpent** Lysander's epithet recalls the image Hermia saw in her nightmare of II.ii.151–52. Compare lines 71–74.

HERMIA   I understand not what you mean by this.
HELENA   I do. Persever, counterfeit Sad Looks;
   Make Mouths upon me when I turn my Back;
   Wink each at other, hold the sweet Jest up.
   This Sport well carried shall be chronicled.   240
   If you have any Pity, Grace, or Manners,
   You would not make me such an Argument.
   But fare ye well; 'tis partly my own Fault,
   Which Death or Absence soon shall remedy.
LYSANDER   Stay, gentle Helena: hear my Excuse,   245
   My Love, my Life, my Soul, fair Helena.
HELENA   O excellent!
HERMIA   Sweet, do not scorn her so.
DEMETRIUS   If she cannot entreat, I can compel.
LYSANDER   Thou canst compel no more than she
      entreat.
   Thy Threats have no more Strength than her weak
      Praise.   250
   Helen, I love thee, by my Life I do;
   I swear by that which I will loose for thee
   To prove him False that says I love thee not.
DEMETRIUS   I say I love thee more than he can do.
LYSANDER   If thou say so, withdraw and prove it too.   255
DEMETRIUS   Quick, come.
HERMIA   Lysander, whereto tends
      all this?
LYSANDER   Away, you Ethiope.
DEMETRIUS   No, no, he'll
   Seem to break loose. Take on as you would follow,
   But yet come not. You are a Tame Man: go.
LYSANDER   Hang off, thou Cat, thou Bur. Vile Thing, let
      loose,   260
   Or I will shake thee from me like a Serpent.

262 **rude** unkind, uncivil, unmannerly. Compare lines 9, 147–48, 182.
Change alteration. Compare II.i.112, 230; II.ii.120; and III.i.115.

263 **tawny Tartar** brown-skinned warrior maiden from central Asia. Lysander is probably punning on *tar*.

265 **sooth** in truth.

267– **Bond . . . Bond** Demetrius plays on two meanings of the word:
68 (a) binding agreement, and (b) restraint (Hermia's clutches). He believes that Lysander is merely pretending to be unable to leave and fight the duel Demetrius has accepted a challenge for. The stunned Hermia probably releases Lysander as she registers what he says in lines 269–70.

272 **what News, my Love?** Suddenly Hermia realizes that Lysander has terrifying news for her: he has not been merely pretending affection for Helena.

274 **ere while** earlier, before.

275 **Since . . . left me** Last night you loved me; yet since last night you've left me.

276 **(O . . . forbid)** Compare the very different tone this kind of expression has in III.i.30 and IV.ii.13–14.

277 **I** Both (a) I [did], and (b) Ay. See note to line 289.

280 **Jest** This noun recalls lines 239, 265.

282 **Juggler** trickster, wanton. Compare *1 Henry VI*, V.vi.68, and *Troilus and Cressida*, II.iii.81–86, V.ii.18.
Canker-Blossom either (a) wild rose, or (b) the larva that destroys a dog-rose in the bud stage. In this line Hermia accuses Helena of using the same criminal methods that Egeus has charged Lysander with in I.i.31–32.

284 **Fine, i'faith** Fine, indeed. Helena assumes that the ruse has simply entered another phase, with Hermia now pretending to believe not only that Lysander loves Helena but that Helena has deliberately stolen his love away from Hermia.

289 **Ay** Here as in lines 237 and 277 the early texts print *I*. Compare II.i.238, 248.

HERMIA   Why are you grown so rude? What Change is this,
  Sweet Love?
LYSANDER   Thy Love? Out, tawny Tartar, out.
  Out, loathed Med'cine. O hated Potion, hence.
HERMIA   Do you not jest?
HELENA   Yes, sooth, and so do you.   265
LYSANDER   Demetrius, I will keep my Word with thee.
DEMETRIUS   I would I had your Bond, for I perceive
  A weak Bond holds you; I'll not trust your Word.
LYSANDER   What, should I hurt her, strike her, kill her dead?
  Although I hate her, I'll not harm her so.   270
HERMIA   What? Can you do me greater Harm than Hate?
  Hate me, wherefore? O me, what News, my Love?
  Am not I Hermia? Are not you Lysander?
  I am as Fair now as I was ere while.
  Since Night you lov'd me; yet since Night you
    left me.   275
  Why then you left me (O, the Gods forbid)
  In earnest, shall I say?
LYSANDER   I, by my Life:
  And never did desire to see thee more.
  Therefore be out of Hope, of Question, of Doubt.
  Be certain, nothing truer: 'tis no Jest   280
  That I do hate thee and love Helena.
HERMIA   — O me, you Juggler, you Canker-Blossom,
  You Thief of Love. What, have you come by Night
  And stol'n my Love's Heart from him?
HELENA   Fine, i' faith.
  Have you no Modesty, no Maiden Shame,   285
  No touch of Bashfulness? What, will you tear
  Impatient Answers from my gentle Tongue?
  Fie, fie, you Counterfeit, you Puppet you.
HERMIA   Puppet? Why so! Ay, that way goes the Game.

92

291   **urg'd**   put forward as a point in a debate.

292   **Personage**   In this line the differing metrical positions give this word slightly varying pronunciations: (a) Pers'nage, and (b) Personage.

295   **Low**   short.

296   **painted**   cosmetically enhanced (like the 'Juggler' you are). Compare the derogatory references to *painting* in *Hamlet*, III.i.145–49, and *Measure for Measure*, III.i.368.
      Maypole   Hermia alludes not only to Helena's tall, skinny stature, but also to the licentiousness associated with May Day celebrations. Compare I.i.165–68 and IV.i.135–37.

300   **Curst**   shrewish, fierce, ungovernable. Compare line 323.

302   **right Maid**   very maid, true maid; *right* is used here primarily for emphasis. *Maid* recalls II.ii.65.

304   **something lower**   somewhat shorter.

305   **match her**   combat with her on equal terms, if not terms to my own advantage. *Match* can also mean 'be paired with', a reminder of lines 198–219.

308   **Did ever keep your Counsels**   kept your confidences, was faithful to you.

312   **chid**   chided, scolded.

313   **spurn me**   shove me away with his foot. Compare II.i.205.

317   **Simple**   innocent, guileless. Compare V.i.83.
      Fond   foolish. This word recalls II.ii.94.

     – Now I perceive that she hath made compare   290
     Between our Statures: she hath urg'd her Height;
     And with her Personage, her tall Personage,
     Her Height, forsooth, she hath prevail'd with him.
     – And are you grown so High in his Esteem
     Because I am so Dwarfish and so Low?   295
     How Low am I, thou painted Maypole? Speak:
     How Low am I? I am not yet so Low
     But that my Nails can reach unto thine Eyes.
HELENA   I pray you, though you mock me, Gentlemen,
     Let her not hurt me. I was never Curst;   300
     I have no gift at all in Shrewishness;
     I am a right Maid for my Cowardice.
     Let her not strike me. You perhaps may think,
     Because she is something lower than my self,
     That I can match her.
HERMIA   Lower? Hark, again.   305
HELENA   Good Hermia, do not be so bitter with me:
     I evermore did love you, Hermia,
     Did ever keep your Counsels, never wrong'd you,
     Save that in love unto Demetrius
     I told him of your Stealth unto this Wood.   310
     He followed you; for Love I followed him.
     But he hath chid me hence, and threat'ned me
     To strike me, spurn me, nay to kill me too.
     And now, so you will let me quiet go,
     To Athens will I bear my Folly back,   315
     And follow you no further. Let me go:
     You see how Simple and how Fond I am.
HERMIA   Why, get you gone. Who is't that hinders
     you?
HELENA   A foolish Heart, that I leave here behind.
HERMIA   What, with Lysander?
HELENA   With Demetrius.   320
LYSANDER   Be not afraid: she shall not harm thee,
     Helena.

94

322   **though . . . part**   either (a) even if you side with her, or (b) even
      though you are defending her. Demetrius' words suggest that
      Lysander is now holding Hermia (to keep her from attacking
      Helena), an amusing reversal of the previous situation but one
      that makes Demetrius assume that he is still evading a duel.
      Another possibility is that Lysander is now being clutched by
      Helena, or perhaps shielding Helena from Hermia's threats.

323   **Shrewd**   shrewish, ill-tempered; beshrewed (cursed). Compare
      line 300, and see II.i.33 and II.ii.60. Sometimes *shrewd* is
      spelled *shrew'd* in the early texts.

327   **flout**   scorn, mock.

329   **Minimus**   Latin for *least*; tiniest of things.
      Knotgrass   a creeping weed thought to hinder the growth of
      one who consumed it. *Hind'ring* echoes line 318.

330   **officious**   dutiful, solicitous.

334   **Never**   Modern usage would call for *ever* here.
      Shew   Show. Compare II.ii.110–11.

335   **aby**   buy, pay dearly, regret. This verb echoes line 175.

336– **to try whose Right . . . is most in Helena**   Lysander assumes
37   that a trial by combat will test the rightness of the lover's
      respective claims on Helena's affections.

338   **Follow? . . . Jowl.**   In this line the actor playing Demetrius
      would stress the word *with*.

339   **Coil**   turmoil. Compare *Romeo and Juliet*, II.iv.66.
      long of you   belongs to you, is because of you.

341   **curst**   probably both shrewish and cursed. Compare lines 300,
      323.

344   **amaz'd**   astonished, bewildered, in a maze. This word echoes
      line 220.

345   **still**   either (a) even yet (the usual modern meaning of *still*), or
      (b) ever.
      mistak'st   This word echoes line 80. Compare line 347.

347   **Shadows**   a reference to the Fairies' invisibility. This word will
      recur in V.i.118, 447.

DEMETRIUS   No Sir, she shall not, though you take
   her part.
HELENA   O when she is Angry, she is Keen and Shrewd.
   She was a Vixen when she went to School;
   And though she be but Little, she is Fierce.   325
HERMIA   Little again? Nothing but Low and Little?
   Why will you suffer her to flout me thus?
   Let me come to her.
LYSANDER   Get you gone, you Dwarf.
   You Minimus of hind'ring Knotgrass made;
   You Bead, you Acorn.
DEMETRIUS   You are too officious   330
   In her behalf that scorns your Services.
   Let her alone: speak not of Helena,
   Take not her part; for if thou dost intend
   Never so little shew of Love to her,
   Thou shalt aby it.
LYSANDER   Now she holds me not: 335
   Now follow, if thou dar'st, to try whose Right,
   Of thine or mine, is most in Helena.
DEMETRIUS   Follow? Nay: I'll go with thee, Cheek by
   Jowl.   *Exeunt Lysander and Demetrius.*
HERMIA   You, Mistress, all this Coil is long of you.
   Nay, go not back.
HELENA   I will not trust you, I,   340
   Nor longer stay in your curst Company.
   Your Hands than mine are quicker for a Fray;
   My Legs are longer, though, to run away.
HERMIA   I am amaz'd, and know not what to say.
                    Exeunt [Helena, then Hermia].
OBERON   This is thy Negligence: still thou
   mistak'st,   345
   Or else commit'st thy Knaveries wilfully.
PUCK   Believe me, King of Shadows, I mistook:
   Did you not tell me I should know the Man

352 **sort**   sort out, occur

353 **As**   that. So also in line 359.
  Jangling   quarrelling, wrangling. The sound of the word is
    meant to imitate a harsh, discordant noise, as of a bell out of
    tune. *Sport* echoes line 240.

355 **Hie**   hasten.
  overcast   over-cast; cover with clouds.

356 **Welkin**   curved vault of the heavens; the sky.

357 **Acheron**   one of the four rivers of Hades. Here the word alludes
    to Hell itself.

360 **frame**   fashion, mould.

361 **Wrong**   insult, slander.

362 **rail**   shout scornful denunciations.

365 **batty**   batlike. Compare II.ii.4–5.

366 **crush**   squeeze.

367 **Liquor**   liquid. Compare II.i.178.
  virtuous Property   powerful quality.

368 **Error**   both (a) mistakes, and (b) wandering (the original sense).
    Compare line 381, and II.ii.41.

369 **wonted**   accustomed, normal. Compare I.i.215, II.i.113.

370 **Derision**   Pronounced with four syllables; similarly, *Vision* in
    the next line is spoken with three syllables (víz-ee-on).

371 **fruitless**   bearing no offspring, having no consequences.

372 **wend**   go.

373 **League**   union. Compare I.i.159.
  Date   duration.

380 **Aurora's Harbinger**   the Morning Star, precursor of the
    Goddess of Dawn.

By the Athenian Garments he had on?
And so far blameless proves my Enterprise   350
That I have 'nointed an Athenian's Eyes;
And so far am I glad it so did sort,
As this their Jangling I esteem a Sport.
OBERON   Thou seest these Lovers seek a place to
   fight:
  Hie therefore, Robin, overcast the Night;   355
  The starry Welkin cover thou anon
  With drooping Fog as black as Acheron,
  And lead these testy Rivals so astray
  As one come not within another's way.
  Like to Lysander sometime frame thy Tongue;   360
  Then stir Demetrius up with bitter Wrong.
  And sometime rail thou like Demetrius;
  And from each other look thou lead them thus,
  Till o'er their Brows Death-counterfeiting Sleep
  With leaden Legs and batty Wings doth creep.   365
  Then crush this Herb into Lysander's Eye,
  Whose Liquor hath this virtuous Property,
  To take from thence all Error with his Might
  And make his Eyeballs roll with wonted Sight.
  When they next wake, all this Derision   370
  Shall seem a Dream and fruitless Vision,
  And back to Athens shall the Lovers wend
  With League whose Date till Death shall never
    end.
  Whiles I in this Affair do thee employ,
  I'll to my Queen and beg her Indian Boy,   375
  And then I will her charmed Eye release
  From Monster's view, and all things shall be
    Peace.
PUCK   My Fairy Lord, this must be done with haste,
  For Night's swift Dragons cut the Clouds full
    fast
  And yonder shines Aurora's Harbinger,   380

383   **in Cross-ways**   at crossroads.
       Floods   rivers and other bodies of water. Suicides and other
       'Damned Spirits' were often buried at crossroads, unless they
       drowned themselves and were washed away by the stream.

384   **wormy Beds**   graves.

385   **least**   lest, unless. Compare III.ii.175.

387   **consort . . . Night**   It was commonly assumed that the ghosts of
       the damned moved about only at night. *Aye* recalls I.i.71, 90.

388   **Spirits of another sort**   Shakespeare wants to make it clear that
       the Fairies in *A Midsummer Night's Dream* are not to be
       thought of as evil spirits. *Sport* recalls line 240.

390   **Forester**   the warden or keeper of protected parks or hunting
       preserves (forests) for the nobility.

391   **Eastern Gate**   the gateway of the rising Sun.

392   **Neptune**   the sea, here designated by the name of its presiding
       deity. Compare II.i.126.

402   **Here, Villain**   As he speaks this line, Robin (Puck) imitates
       Demetrius' voice.

403   **straight**   directly, forthwith; straightway.

404   **plainer Ground**   clearer ground, with fewer obstructions and
       less vegetation; ground where you won't be able to hide
       yourself from me.

At whose approach Ghosts wand'ring here and
  there
Troop home to Churchyards. Damned Spirits all,
That in Cross-ways and Floods have burial,
Already to their wormy Beds are gone:
For fear least Day should look their Shames upon,   385
They wilfully themselves exile from Light,
And must for aye consort with black-brow'd Night.
OBERON   But we are Spirits of another sort:
  I with the Morning's Love have oft made sport,
  And like a Forester the Groves may tread   390
  Even till the Eastern Gate all fiery red,
  Opening on Neptune with fair blessed Beams,
  Turns into yellow Gold his salt green Streams.
  But notwithstanding, haste, make no Delay:
  We may effect this Business yet ere Day.   [*Exit.*]   395
PUCK   Up and down, up and down;
    I will lead them up and down;
    I am fear'd in Field and Town.
    Goblin, lead them up and down.
  Here comes one.   400

Enter Lysander.

LYSANDER   Where art thou, proud Demetrius?
    Speak thou now.
ROBIN   Here, Villain, drawn and ready. Where art
    thou?
LYSANDER   I will be with thee straight.
ROBIN   Follow me then
    To plainer Ground.

Enter Demetrius.

DEMETRIUS   Lysander, speak again.
    Thou Runaway, thou Coward, art thou fled?   405

406 **Speak ... Bush** This sentence is here reproduced as it appears
in the Quarto and Folio printings. Most editors revise it to
read: 'Speak! In some bush?' The implication of the original
punctuation is that Demetrius expects Lysander to be hiding
in a bush, a sense compatible with the tone of his remarks in
lines 256–59, 267–68. Lysander may be alluding satirically to
Moses' encounter with the burning bush in Exodus 3:4, where
'God called unto him out of the midst of the bush, and said,
Moses, Moses. And he said, Here am I.' *Bush* recalls
III.i.59–62 and anticipates V.i.137, 259–61.

408 **thou look'st for Wars** you are a 'wand'ring Knight' (I.ii.46) in
quest of opportunities to display your prowess in heroic
combat.

409 **Recreant** traitor, craven coward.

410–11 **he is defil'd ... thee** Robin says that Demetrius is so lacking in
manly courage that it would dishonour an opponent to treat
him other than as a naughty child.

412 **try no Manhood here** put no honour to the trial in this place.
Compare lines 254–56, 355–59.

415 **lighter-heel'd** This phrase, alluding perhaps to the fleet-footed
Atalanta, echoes lines 340–43. Ovid had told Atalanta's story
in Books VIII and X of the *Metamorphoses*.

417 **in dark Uneven Way** in a dark, rough terrain. Lysander's
words echo the opening lines of Dante's *Inferno*, where the
narrator describes himself as 'in a dark wood where the
straight way was lost' (Temple Classics translation).

422 **Abide me** stay for me.
wot know.

423 **shifting every place** Demetrius' phrasing recalls the shifting
voice of the Ghost in the 'Cellarage' in *Hamlet*, I.v.144–55.

426 **buy this dear** pay dearly for this. Compare lines 175, 335.

428 **constraineth** forces. *Faintness* recalls II.ii.41.

429 **measure ... Bed** Demetrius' phrasing is similar to Romeo's in
III.iii.65–70 of *Romeo and Juliet*.

430 **By Day's approach ... visited** When day comes, be prepared
for me to find you.

Speak in some Bush. Where dost thou hide thy
    Head?
ROBIN   Thou Coward, art thou bragging to the Stars,
    Telling the Bushes that thou look'st for Wars,
    And wilt not come? Come, Recreant; come, thou
    Child.
    I'll whip thee with a Rod: he is defil'd   410
    That draws a Sword on thee.
DEMETRIUS   Yea, art thou there?
ROBIN   Follow my Voice: we'll try no Manhood here.
                                              Exeunt.
LYSANDER   He goes before me and still dares me on:
    When I come where he calls, then he is gone.
    The Villain is much lighter-heel'd than I.   415
    I follow'd fast, but faster he did fly,   *Shifting places*
    That fallen am I in dark Uneven Way,
    And here will rest me.   *Lie down.*
              – Come, thou gentle Day:
    For if but once thou shew me thy grey Light,
    I'll find Demetrius and revenge this Spight.   420

            [*Enter*] *Robin and Demetrius.*

PUCK   Ho, ho, ho: Coward, why com'st thou not?
DEMETRIUS   Abide me if thou dar'st: for well I wot
    Thou runn'st before me, shifting every place,
    And dar'st not stand, nor look me in the Face.
    Where art thou now?
ROBIN   Come hither: I am here.   425
DEMETRIUS   Nay, then thou mock'st me. Thou shalt
    buy this dear
    If ever I thy Face by Daylight see.
    Now go thy way. Faintness constraineth me
    To measure out my Length on this cold Bed.
    By Day's approach look to be visited.   430
                                          [*Lie down.*]

432　**Abate**　diminish or end. Line 431 anticipates V.i.172–74, where Shakespeare burlesques the trials of Helena and her companions. *Comforts* recalls II.ii.43–44.

435　**Sorrow's Eye**　Lines 435–36 echo lines 82–87.

437　**Come one more**　either (a) 'Let one more come', or (b) 'Come, one more'.

439　**curst**　shrewish, angry. Compare line 341.

440　**knavish**　wicked, mischievous. Robin's adjective calls to mind Bottom's remarks in III.i.113–14, 121–22.

441　**mad**　distracted (see III.ii.31). But here the modern sense (angry) is also pertinent.

445　**Desires**　This word recalls the play's opening speech (I.i.1–6). Compare I.i.67, 127; III.i.153; III.ii.278.

447　**mean a Fray**　intend to fight a duel. Hermia doesn't realize that she is now resting adjacent to Lysander, and that he, Demetrius, and Helena are already asleep. As soon as she lies down, Robin enters to put on Lysander's eyelids the antidote to the charm that has made him fall in love with Helena (see lines 366–74).

452　**Gentle Lover**　Lysander.

458　**Country Proverb known**　well-known country proverb. The reverse word order is for rhyming purposes in what may have been performed as a chant or song.

Enter Helena.

HELENA   O weary Night, O long and tedious Night,
   Abate thy Hours, shine Comforts from the East,
   That I may back to Athens by Day-light
   From these that my poor Company detest.
   – And Sleep, that sometimes shuts up Sorrow's Eye,   435
   Steal me a while from mine own Company.

                                            Sleep.

ROBIN   Yet but three? Come one more:
   Two of both kinds make up four.

Enter Hermia.

   Here she comes, curst and sad;
   Cupid is a knavish Lad   440
   Thus to make poor Females mad.
HERMIA   Never so Weary, never so in Woe,
   Bedabbled with the Dew, and torn with Briers:
   I can no further crawl, no further go,
   My Legs can keep no pace with my Desires.   445
   Here will I rest me till the break of Day;
   Heavens shield Lysander if they mean a Fray.

                                        [*Sleep.*]

ROBIN   On the Ground
   Sleep sound.
   I'll apply   450
   To your Eye,
   Gentle Lover, Remedy.
   When thou wak'st,
   Thou tak'st
   True Delight   455
   In the Sight
   Of thy former Lady's Eye.
   And the Country Proverb known,
   That every Man should take his own,

463 **Mare** woman. The word *Mare* alliterates with *Man*, and may also have been chosen because of its rustic flavour.

S.D. **[Exit]** In the First Folio printing of the play, the scene ends with the notation that 'They sleepe all the Act'. What this probably means is that the lovers remain on the stage, asleep and in full view of the audience, until they are awakened by Theseus' horns at IV.i.141.

464 **And . . . well** This line echoes Oberon's concluding words in line 377.

In your Waking shall be shown.   460
    Jack shall have Jill;
    Nought shall go ill;
The Man shall have his Mare again,
And all shall be well.

[*Exit.*]

IV.i   The setting remains the wood, but Titania's company is now
closer to the area occupied by the lovers. The 'Clown' of the
opening stage direction is Bottom. Shakespeare often uses this
generic label, probably because he is thinking of the actor
(Will Kemp) who plays bumpkins.

2   **amiable** loveable.
coy caress, cuddle. Titania's verb comes from the vocabulary
of falconry.

8   **Mounsieur** The spelling reflects Bottom's pronunciation. We
should of course note how polite and magnanimous Bottom is
in his new role as consort of the Fairy Queen.

14   **fret** trouble.
Action performing of the deed. Bottom's phrasing suggests that
Cobweb's exploit will involve high drama. It is not clear
whether Cobweb exits to fulfil Bottom's wishes. The early
texts provide no exit, nor do most modern editions supply
one.

15   **have a care** be careful.

16   **be loath** hate.

17   **overflowen with** soaked with.

20   **Neaf** hand; fist.

21   **leave your Curtsy** stop bowing in deference. Bottom may also
be telling Mustardseed that he can put his hat back on his
head.

24   **Cavalery** *Cavaliere*, an Italian gentleman; like *Signior* (line 17)
and *Mounsieur* (line 10), this is an expression of respect.

ACT IV

Scene 1

Enter Queen of Fairies, and Clown, and Fairies; and the King behind them.

TITANIA   Come, sit thee down upon this flow'ry Bed
   While I thy amiable Cheeks do coy,
   And stick Musk-roses in thy sleek, smooth Head,
   And kiss thy fair large Ears, my gentle Joy.
CLOWN   Where's Peaseblossom?   5
PEASEBLOSSOM   Ready.
CLOWN   Scratch my Head, Peaseblossom. – Where's
   Mounsieur Cobweb?
COBWEB   Ready.
CLOWN   Mounsieur Cobweb, good Mounsieur, get you   10
   your Weapons in your Hand and kill me a red-
   hipp'd Humble-bee on the top of a Thistle; and
   good Mounsieur, bring me the Honeybag. Do not
   fret yourself too much in the Action, Mounsieur;
   and good Mounsieur, have a care the Honeybag   15
   break not: I would be loath to have you
   overflowen with a Honeybag, Signior.
   – Where's Mounsieur Mustardseed?
MUSTARDSEED   Ready.
CLOWN   Give me your Neaf, Mounsieur Mustardseed.   20
   Pray you leave your Curtsy, good Mounsieur.
MUSTARDSEED   What's your will?
CLOWN   Nothing, good Mounsieur, but to help
   Cavalery Cobweb to scratch. I must to the

26   **marvailes** Bottom's pronunciation of *marvellous*. Compare
      III.i.2.

31   **Tongs** rustic metal instruments, struck with a key as a triangle
      is struck today.
      Bones clappers of bone or wood, rattled together with the
      hands. After this line the First Folio adds a stage direction
      '*Music Tongs, Rural Music*'.

33   **Provender** livestock fodder. An amusing reminder of Bottom's
      'Mortal Grossness' (III.i.161) in contrast to Titania's refined
      delicacy. A *peck* is a half bushel (two gallons in dry measure),
      here one for Bottom to peck at.
      mounch Bottom's pronunciation of *munch*.

35   **bottle** bundle. *Desire* echoes III.ii.445.

37   **Hoord** hoard.

41   **Exposition of Sleep** An *exposition* is an explanation; Bottom is
      again trying to mimic the speech of his social superiors, who
      would probably have said 'Disposition to sleep' here. By the
      end of the scene, however, Bottom will indeed provide 'an
      Exposition of Sleep' (lines 206–23). In his epilogue
      (V.ii.53–68) Puck will invite the audience to do the same
      thing, on the assumption that we, like Bottom, 'have but
      slumb'red here'.

44   **always away** Most editors emend the *alwaies* of the Quarto
      and Folio texts to *all ways*, on the assumption that Titania
      means for her elves to disperse in different directions. It seems
      much more in character for her at this moment to mean
      'always' – to get lost and stay lost until the Fairy Queen
      summons them back. She wants to be left completely alone
      with the paragon she dotes upon, and she is eager to comply
      with his every wish, including his request to 'let none of your
      people [attendants] stir me' (lines 40–41).

52   **Favours** love-tokens.
      this hateful Fool this clown, whom she would loathe if she
      were not charmed into 'Dotage' or infatuation.

Barber's, Mounsieur. For me thinks I am   25
marvailes hairy about the Face; and I am such
a tender Ass, if my Hair do but tickle me I
must scratch.

TITANIA What, wilt thou hear some Music, my sweet
   Love?

CLOWN I have a reasonable good Ear in Music. Let's   30
have the Tongs and the Bones.

TITANIA Or say, sweet Love, what thou desirest to
   eat.

CLOWN Truly, a peck of Provender. I could mounch
your good dry Oats. Me thinks I have a great
desire to a bottle of Hay. Good Hay, sweet Hay,   35
hath no Fellow.

TITANIA I have a venturous Fairy that shall seek
The Squirrels Hoord and fetch thee new Nuts.

CLOWN I had rather have a handful or two of
dried Pease. But I pray you let none of your   40
people stir me: I have an Exposition of Sleep
come upon me.

TITANIA Sleep thou, and I will wind thee in my
   Arms.
— Fairies, be gone, and be always away.

                                    [*Exeunt Fairies.*]

— So doth the Woodbine, the sweet Honeysuckle,   45
Gently entwist; the female Ivy so
Enrings the barky Fingers of the Elm.
O how I love thee! How I dote on thee!   [*Sleep.*]

Enter Robin Goodfellow.

OBERON Welcome, good Robin. Seest thou this
   sweet Sight?
Her Dotage now I do begin to pity.   50
For meeting her of late, behind the Wood,
Seeking sweet Favours for this hateful Fool,

56 **Dew** This word recalls II.i.9 and III.ii.443. It also echoes III.ii.214.

57 **orient** lustrous, precious.

58 **Flouriets** flowerets, little flowers.

61 **Patience** Compare III.ii.159–61.

63 **straight** immediately, without argument. Compare III.ii.403.

66 **hateful** loathsome. Compare line 52.

67 **transformed** here pronounced as a three-syllable word. Compare III.ii.32.

68 **Swain** gallant peasant lover.

69 **other** others.

70 **repair** return. But those who return with them will return repaired in crucial respects.

72 **fierce** This word recalls III.ii.82, 325.

74 **Be as thou wast wont to be** Be as you were before. As Oberon speaks there lines, he drops the antidote on Titania's eyelids.

75 **wont** accustomed. Compare III.ii.369.

76–77 **Dian's Bud . . . Power** Just as Cupid's flower induces love, Diana's bud removes it.

85 **of all these, fine the Sense** This is the language found in both the Quarto and the Folio. The word *fine* can be read as either 'end' or 'finish off', and 'of all these, fine the Sense' can thus be interpreted as an amplification of 'strike more dead / Than common Sleep'. Another possible interpretation is that *fine* is an aphetic form of 'refine' or 'purify', which would yield the reading 'of all these, refine the Sense'. Modern editions normally emend *fine* to *five* and delete the Quarto's colon.

I did upbraid her and fall out with her.
For she his hairy Temples then had rounded
With Coronet of fresh and fragrant Flowers.   55
And that same Dew which sometime on the Buds
Was wont to swell like round and orient Pearls
Stood now within the pretty Flouriets' Eyes,
Like Tears that did their own Disgrace bewail.
When I had at my Pleasure taunted her,   60
And she in mild terms begg'd my Patience,
I then did ask of her her Changeling Child,
Which straight she gave me, and her Fairy sent
To bear him to my Bower in Fairy Land.
And now I have the Boy, I will undo   65
This hateful Imperfection of her Eyes.
And gentle Puck, take this transformed Scalp
From off the Head of this Athenian Swain,
That he, awaking when the other do,
May all to Athens back again repair,   70
And think no more of this Night's Accidents
But as the fierce Vexation of a Dream.
But first I will release the Fairy Queen.
   — Be as thou wast wont to be;
   See as thou wast wont to see.   75
   Dian's Bud o'er Cupid's Flower
   Hath such Force and blessed Power.
Now my Titania, wake you, my sweet Queen.
TITANIA   My Oberon, what Visions have I seen!
Me thought I was enamour'd of an Ass.   80
OBERON   There lies your Love.
TITANIA   How came these things to pass?
   O, how mine Eyes do loathe his Visage now!
OBERON   Silence a while. — Robin, take off this Head.
   — Titania, Music call, and strike more dead
Than common Sleep: of all these, fine the Sense.   85
TITANIA   Music, ho Music: such as charmeth Sleep.
                                        Music still.

90   **Amity**   cordiality, love. Compare line 2.

98   **sad**   solemn.

99   **Night's Shade**   Night's shadow (with an extra vowel to be added to either *Night* or *Shade* to make it a two-syllable word in this metrical context).

100   **Globe**   By the time the first publication of *A Midsummer Night's Dream* appeared in 1600, Shakespeare and his company were compassing a Globe of their own, the playhouse they had opened on Bankside in 1599.
compass   encircle.

101   **wand'ring**   Compare III.ii.368, 381.

107   **Observation**   Theseus may mean 'observance' (see lines 135–37), but he is also referring to his role as a noble lord surveying his estate and showing it to his bride-to-be.

108   **Vaward**   vanguard. Theseus means 'since we are in the earliest part of the day'.

110   **Uncouple**   release them from the restraints holding them together in pairs; allow them to run freely.

115   **Hercules and Cadmus**   legendary heroes. Cadmus was the founder of Thebes.

ROBIN   Now when thou wak'st, with thine own Fool's
   Eyes peep.
OBERON   Sound Music.
          – Come, my Queen, take hands with me,
   And rock the Ground whereon these Sleepers be.
   Now thou and I are new in Amity,   90
   And will to morrow Midnight solemnly
   Daunce in Duke Theseus' House triumphantly
   And bless it to all fair Prosperity.
   There shall the pairs of faithful Lovers be
   Wedded, with Theseus, all in Jollity.   95
ROBIN   Fairy King, attend and mark:
   I do hear the Morning Lark.
OBERON   Then my Queen, in Silence sad
   Trip we after Night's Shade;
   We the Globe can compass soon,   100
   Swifter than the wand'ring Moon.
TITANIA   Come, my Lord, and in our Flight
   Tell me how it came this Night
   That I sleeping here was found
   With these Mortals on the Ground.   105
             [*Exeunt Oberon, Titania, and Robin.*]

   Wind Horn. Enter Theseus and all his Train.

THESEUS   Go, one of you, find out the Forester:
   For now our Observation is perform'd,
   And since we have the Vaward of the Day,
   My Love shall hear the Music of my Hounds.
   Uncouple in the Western Valley, let them go;   110
   Dispatch, I say, and find the Forester.
               [*Exit an Attendant.*]
   – We will, fair Queen, up to the Mountain's Top,
   And mark the Musical Confusion
   Of Hounds and Echo in Conjunction.
HIPPOLYTA   I was with Hercules and Cadmus once   115

118   **gallant Chiding**   Like 'sweet Thunder' in line 121, this linking of seemingly contrary things is part of the 'musical . . . Discord' (line 121) Hippolyta is describing. The literal meaning of *Confusion* (line 113) is 'mix or pour together'.

122   **bred out of the Spartan kind**   bred from Spartan pedigrees.

123   **flew'd**   with the 'flews' or chaps (folds of flesh around the mouth) characteristic of bloodhounds.
        sanded   sand-coloured.

125   **dewlapp'd**   both (a) marked by dewlaps (folds of skin hanging from the throat), and (b) wet with dew from the dogs' running with their noses to the ground in pursuit of the scent of the prey. Compare II.i.50. *Tuneable* recalls I.i.184.

127   **Each under each**   This phrase continues the bell image from the preceding line. Theseus compares the hounds' barking to the sounds of a set of bells arranged to yield a full gamut of tones, from high pitches to low ones.

128   **hollow'd**   hollered, hallooed.

134   **wonder of**   wonder at.

136   **Right**   rite. See the note to I.i.97.

137   **in grace of**   to do honour to.

143   **Woodbirds**   According to tradition, birds chose their mates on St Valentine's Day.

144   **Pardon, my Lord**   The First Quarto and First Folio texts do not provide a question mark here, but Lysander's line is probably to be spoken in puzzlement as the four lovers are rousing themselves from slumber. It may be that they kneel as Lysander speaks these words; but it is also possible that before they have time to show such deference they are told to stand up.

When in a Wood of Crete they bay'd the Bear
With Hounds of Sparta; never did I hear
Such gallant Chiding. For besides the Groves,
The Skies, the Fountains, every Region near
Seem all one Mutual Cry. I never heard   120
So musical a Discord, such sweet Thunder.
THESEUS   My Hounds are bred out of the Spartan kind,
So flew'd, so sanded; and their Heads are hung
With Ears that sweep away the Morning Dew,
Crook-kneed and dewlapp'd, like Thessalian
    Bulls: 125
Slow in Pursuit, but match'd in Mouth like Bells,
Each under each. A Cry more tuneable
Was never hollow'd to, nor cheer'd with Horn,
In Crete, in Sparta, nor in Thessaly.
Judge when you hear. But soft, what Nymphs are
    these?   130
EGEUS   My Lord, this is my Daughter here asleep,
And this Lysander, this Demetrius is,
This Helena, old Nedar's Helena.
I wonder of their being here together.
THESEUS   No doubt they rose up early to observe   135
The Right of May, and hearing our Intent
Came here in grace of our Solemnity.
But speak, Egeus: is not this the Day
That Hermia should give answer of her Choice?
EGEUS   It is, my Lord.   140
THESEUS   Go bid the Huntsmen wake them with their
    Horns.   [*Exit an Attendant.*]

   Shout within: they all start up. Wind Horns.

THESEUS   Good morrow, Friends. Saint Valentine is
    past:
Begin these Wood-birds but to couple now?
LYSANDER   Pardon, my Lord.

147 **Jealousy** suspicion, mistrust.

149 **amazedly** in bewilderment, as by one lost in a maze. Compare III.ii.344.

160 **defeated** frustrated the wishes of; defrauded, denied.

166 **in Fancy** prompted by infatuation. Compare I.i.155, II.i.164. *Fancy* balances *Fury* in the preceding line, to remind us that what drove Demetrius to the wood (hate) has now been defeated by what pulled Helena there (love).

167 **wot** know. Compare III.ii.422.

170 **idle Gaud** trifling plaything. Compare I.i.30–35.

171 **dote upon** idolise. Compare lines 48, 50, and II.i.171.

175 **see** saw. It may be that Demetrius switches to the present tense to convey more vividly the change of heart he experienced upon seeing Hermia. Lines 174–76 recall lines 65–66, 81–82.

THESEUS   I pray you all stand up.
  I know you two are rival Enemies: 145
  How comes this gentle Concord in the World,
  That Hatred is so far from Jealousy
  To sleep by Hate, and fear no Enmity?
LYSANDER   My Lord, I shall reply amazedly,
  Half Sleep, half Waking. But as yet I swear   150
  I cannot truly say how I came here.
  But as I think (for truly would I speak),
  And now I do bethink me, so it is:
  I came with Hermia hither. Our Intent
  Was to be gone from Athens, where we might   155
  Without the peril of the Athenian Law –
EGEUS   Enough, enough, my Lord; you have enough.
  I beg the Law, the Law, upon his Head.
  – They would have stol'n away, they would,
    Demetrius,
  Thereby to have defeated you and me: 160
  You of your Wife, and me of my Consent,
  Of my Consent that she should be your Wife.
DEMETRIUS   My Lord, fair Helen told me of their
    Stealth,
  Of this their Purpose hither to this Wood;
  And I in Fury hither followed them,   165
  Fair Helena in Fancy following me.
  But my good Lord, I wot not by what Power
  (But by some Power it is), my Love to Hermia,
  Melted as the Snow, seems to me now
  As the Remembrance of an idle Gaud   170
  Which in my Childhood I did dote upon;
  And all the Faith, the Virtue of my Heart,
  The Object and the Pleasure of mine Eye,
  Is only Helena. To her, my Lord,
  Was I betroth'd ere I see Hermia,   175
  But like a Sickness did I loathe this Food;
  But as in Health, come to my Natural Taste,

180   **fortunately met**   brought together in a way that augurs well for your love.

182   **Egeus, I will overbear your Will**   In the opening scene of the play, Theseus represented himself as unable to 'extenuate' the Athenian law. But he now seems to recognise a higher 'Power' (line 167) that has returned Demetrius to 'Health' and to his 'Natural Taste' (line 177). In effect, Theseus acknowledges that Demetrius has resolved the initial conflict by removing himself from contention as a suitor for Hermia. Demetrius is now determined to abide by his earlier betrothal contract with Helena, and Theseus would be failing to uphold another Athenian law if he now insisted on enforcing Egeus' 'Will'. Whether Egeus accepts this outcome without rancour is left for each interpreter of the play to decide; the text is mute. At this point Egeus disappears from the Quarto version of the play. In the Folio version, however, he reappears in Act V as Master of the Revels, replacing the Quarto's Philostrate.

184   **knit**   This verb recalls I.i.172.

185   **for**   because.

190   **These things . . . undistinguishable**   Referring to the events of the previous evening, Demetrius says he now has trouble visualising them, as one does things 'far-off' (line 191). Compare II.i.99–100 and II.ii.60–61.

192   **parted**   divided. Compare III.ii.208–11.

195–   **Are . . . awake?**   This sentence does not appear in the First
96   Folio, perhaps because it is redundant and metrically uncertain and was marked for deletion in the manuscript.

201   **by the way**   on the way.

203   **When my Cue comes**   Bottom (again designated as 'Clown' in the speech heading) is returned to where he was before he was charmed. What happened during the night is now reduced – for him and for the lovers – to the aspect of a dream. Compare the comments Hermia makes as she emerges from her dream in II.ii.151–52. *Cue* echoes III.i.75–77, 99–101.

Now I do wish it, love it, long for it,
And will for evermore be true to it.
THESEUS   Fair Lovers, you are fortunately met;   180
Of this Discourse we more will hear anon.
– Egeus, I will overbear your Will:
For in the Temple by and by with us
These Couples shall eternally be knit.
And, for the Morning now is something worn,   185
Our purpos'd Hunting shall be set aside.
– Away with us to Athens. Three and three
We'll hold a Feast in great Solemnity.
– Come, Hippolyta.   *Exeunt Duke and Lords.*
DEMETRIUS   These things seem small and
   undistinguishable,   190
Like far-off Mountains turned into Clouds.
HERMIA   Me thinks I see these things with parted Eye,
When every thing seems Double.
HELENA   So me thinks;
And I have found Demetrius like a Jewel:
Mine own, and not mine own.
DEMETRIUS   Are you sure   195
That we are awake? It seems to me
That yet we Sleep, we Dream. Do not you think
The Duke was here and bid us follow him?
HERMIA   Yea, and my Father.
HELENA   And Hippolyta.
LYSANDER   And he did bid us follow to the Temple.   200
DEMETRIUS   Why then we are Awake: let's follow him,
And by the way let us recount our Dreams.
                                   Exeunt Lovers.

                    Bottom wakes.

CLOWN   When my Cue comes, call me
   and I will answer. My next is 'Most fair Pyramus'.
Hey ho, Peter Quince? Flute the Bellows-   205

213 **patch'd a Fool** This phrasing is found in the First Quarto text;
the First Folio reads 'a patch'd fool'. Court fools of the time
wore a particoloured costume, and the fool who served
Cardinal Wolsey was even known as 'Patch'. Puck calls
Bottom and his fellow rustics 'Patches' at II.ii.9.

214– **The Eye of Man ... what my Dream was** Bottom's exposition
18 of his 'most rare Vision' (line 207) is a garbled rephrasing of 1
Corinthians 2:9 'Eye hath not seen, nor ear heard, neither
have entered into the heart of man, the things which God hath
prepared for them that love him.' In the 1557 Geneva Bible's
version of the passage, Shakespeare would have found a
sentence in the following verse that may have been a factor in
the choice of 'Bottom' as his name for the sublimest bumpkin
of them all: 'But God hath opened them unto us by his Sprite,
for the Spirite searcheth all things, yea, the bottom of Goddes
secrets.' Bottom's epiphany (see the note to line 41) also calls
to mind such biblical passages as Psalm 8:2, Matthew 21:16,
and especially 1 Corinthians 1:19, 25–31, where we read that
'God hath chosen the foolish things of the world to confound
the wise; and God hath chosen the weak things of the world
to confound the things which are mighty; And base things of
the world, and things which are despised, hath God chosen,
yea, and things which are not to bring to nought things that
are.'

219 **Ballet** Bottom's pronunciation of *ballad*.

222 **Peradventure** perhaps. Bottom's reference to 'a Play' suggests
that he expects to be presenting a full repertory 'before the
Duke'; but 'at her Death' probably indicates that he is
thinking of Thisby's demise.

IV.ii With this scene we return to Athens, to the same setting as in I.ii.
Throughout this scene Flute is designated as Thisby in both
the Quarto and the Folio. The Folio corrects the Quarto's
speech designation for the second speech, which the Quarto
assigns to Flute. The 'Thisby' speech headings suggest that
Flute is already costumed here as the character he will
perform in the play.

3 **heard of** heard from.
Out of doubt undoubtedly.

4 **transported** Starveling means 'taken away', but he unwittingly
speaks correctly about Bottom's 'transported' state under
Puck's charm. Compare I.i.191, III.i.120, III.ii.32, IV.i.67.

mender? Snout the Tinker? Starveling? God's my
life! Stol'n hence, and left me asleep? I have
had a most rare Vision. I have had a Dream –
past the wit of Man to say, what Dream it was.
Man is but an Ass if he go about to expound   210
this Dream. Me thought I was – there is no Man
can tell what. Me thought I was, and me thought
I had – But Man is but patch'd a Fool if he will
offer to say what me thought I had. The Eye of
Man hath not heard, the Ear of Man hath not   215
seen, Man's Hand is not able to taste, his
Tongue to conceive, nor his Heart to report,
what my Dream was. I will get Peter Quince to
write a Ballet of this Dream. It shall be
call'd 'Bottom's Dream', because it hath no   220
Bottom. And I will sing it in the latter end
of a Play, before the Duke. Peradventure to
make it the more gracious, I shall sing it at
her Death.   *Exit.*

Scene 2

Enter Quince, Thisby, Snout, and Starveling.

QUINCE   Have you sent to Bottom's House? Is he come
home yet?
STARVELING   He cannot be heard of. Out of doubt he
is transported.

8   **discharge**   execute. Quince means 'perform', but another sense
        ('kill') is also applicable. Compare I.ii.94 and V.i.207–18.

9   **Wit**   applied intelligence, know-how. But like *Will*, *Wit* can also
        have a genital sense. See the note to III.i.135.

11   **Person**   physical attributes. Here it is hard not to be reminded
        of that part of a man's 'person' that seeks to 'discharge' itself.
        Compare lines 38–39.

12   **Paramour**   sexual partner (used especially of the men and
        women who serve royalty or the nobility as lovers and
        mistresses). Quince speaks more accurately than he realises
        when he describes Bottom as 'a very Paramour, for a sweet
        Voice' (compare III.i.130–206).

14   **thing of Nought**   naughty thing (a stronger term then than
        now). The Quarto spelling turns this particular 'Paramour'
        into what the Prince calls 'a thing . . . Of Nothing' in *Hamlet*,
        IV.ii.29–31. Compare V.i.14–17.

18   **Made Men**   established men; that is, rich men, 'made for life'.
        Sport recalls III.i.14, 119, III.ii.14, 119, 240.

20   **Sixpence a Day**   Sixpence was as much as twice what an
        average artisan would have earned for a day's labour in
        Shakespeare's England.
        during his Life   for the rest of his life.

21   **And**   if. Given the way 'Pyramus' has now been defined, Flute's
        conviction that Bottom would have received 'Sixpence a Day,
        for playing Pyramus' suggests that a 'Made Man' could have
        become 'a thing of nought' indeed if only 'our Sport had gone
        forward' (line 17, echoing III.ii.119). In similar fashion, 'every
        Man look o'er his Part' – especially when juxtaposed with
        'For the short and the long' – is inadvertently bawdy.

26   **Harts**   Bottom probably means 'hearts', but *Harts* (frequently
        symbolising royalty or nobility in Shakespeare) would fit the
        context too. The Folio prints 'hearts', and editors normally
        follow suit. Again, an audience would perceive no distinction.

27   **courageous**   Without realizing it, Quince plays on the Latin
        word for heart, *cor*, from which *courageous* derives.

THISBY   If he come not, then the Play is marr'd. It   5
goes not forward. Doth it?

QUINCE   It is not possible. You have not a Man, in
all Athens, able to discharge Pyramus, but he.

THISBY   No, he hath simply the best Wit of any
Handicraftman in Athens.   10

QUINCE   Yea, and the best Person too, and he is a
very Paramour, for a sweet Voice.

THISBY   You must say Paragon. A Paramour is (God
bless us) a thing of Nought.

Enter Snug, the Joiner.

SNUG   Masters, the Duke is coming from the Temple,   15
and there is two or three Lords and Ladies more
married. If our Sport had gone forward, we had
all been Made Men.

THISBY   O sweet bully Bottom. Thus hath he lost
Sixpence a Day, during his Life; he could not   20
have scaped Sixpence a Day. And the Duke had
not given him Sixpence a Day, for playing
Pyramus, I'll be hanged. He would have deserved
it: Sixpence a Day, in Pyramus, or nothing.

Enter Bottom.

BOTTOM   Where are these Lads? Where are these   25
Harts?

QUINCE   Bottom, O most courageous Day! O most
happy Hour!

BOTTOM   Masters, I am to discourse Wonders: but ask
me not what. For if I tell you, I am not true   30
Athenian. I will tell you every thing right as
it fell out.

QUINCE   Let us hear, sweet Bottom.

BOTTOM   Not a Word of me. All that I will tell you,

35   **dined**   completed his main, midday meal. It is now early
     afternoon. By the time the Mechanicals perform their play,
     the Duke and his court will have also finished supper
     (V.i.31–34).

36   **Strings to your Beards**   strings to hold your stage beards in
     place.

37   **Ribands**   ribbons.
     Pumps   light shoes, normally worn in masques or comedies,
     and thus ironically appropriate for this 'very tragical Mirth'
     (V.i.57).

39   **our Play is preferr'd**   Bottom assumes that their play has
     already been selected for presentation; we soon find out that it
     is simply among the four offered to Theseus as possibilities,
     and that it is anything *but* preferred by Philostrate
     (V.i.77–78).

is that the Duke hath dined. Get your Apparel   35
together, good Strings to your Beards, new
Ribands to your Pumps, meet presently at the
Palace, every Man look o'er his Part. For the
short and the long is, our Play is preferr'd.
In any case let Thisby have clean Linen. And   40
let not him, that plays the Lion, pare his Nails:
for they shall hang out for the Lion's Claws.
And most dear Actors, eat no Onions, nor Garlic:
for we are to utter Sweet Breath. And I do not
doubt but to hear them say, it is a Sweet Comedy.   45
No more Words. Away, go away.   *Exeunt.*

126

V.i We now return to Theseus' palace, where the play began.

2 **may** can.

3 **antique** both (a) ancient, and (b) antic (grotesque and idiotic).
   Toys trifles. Compare I.i.28–35.

4 **seething** agitated, boiling out of the control of 'cool Reason'
   (line 6). Compare line 12.

5 **Phantasies** fantasies. This word recalls II.i.258.
   apprehend conceive; intuit imaginatively. Theseus regards
   apprehension as a less trustworthy capacity than the
   comprehension (line 6), the secure grasp of understanding,
   that he associates with 'Reason' and its dispassionate
   self-discipline. Compare lines 18–20.

8 **compact** composed, made. This word may also be meant to
   imply that those who enter into a subversive 'compact' (plot
   or conspiracy) are likely to have the 'seething Brains' of those
   who let their wild imaginations carry them away. As Caesar
   notes of Cassius in I.ii.191 of *Julius Caesar*, 'He thinks too
   much: such Men are Dangerous'.

9 **Divels** the most common Shakespearean spelling for 'devils'.

11 **Sees ... Egypt** is unable to distinguish the fair complexion of a
   Greek blonde from the dark complexion of an Egyptian.

12 **fine Frenzy** poetic rapture, inspiration. Here *fine* may carry
   sarcastic overtones, as in III.ii.284 and V.i.364.
   rolling here the word suggests a rolling boil.

14 **bodies forth** gives bodily shape to, or gives birth to.

16 **airy Nothing** This phrase is probably meant derogatorily by
   Theseus, who has little use for insubstantial fancies. Compare
   IV.ii.13–14.

20 **comprehends** encompasses, includes in its conception. Line 19
   parallels 'airy Nothing' (line 16); line 20 parallels 'local
   Habitation' (line 17). Compare lines 5–6.

ACT V

Scene 1

Enter Theseus, Hippolyta, and Philostrate
[followed by Lords and Attendants].

HIPPOLYTA   'Tis Strange, my Theseus, that these
    Lovers speak of.
THESEUS   More Strange than True: I never may
    believe
These antique Fables, nor these Fairy Toys.
Lovers and Madmen have such seething Brains,
Such shaping Phantasies, that apprehend   5
More than cool Reason ever comprehends.
The Lunatic, the Lover, and the Poet
Are of Imagination all compact.
One sees more Divels than vast Hell can hold:
That is the Madman. The Lover, all as frantic,   10
Sees Helen's Beauty in a Brow of Egypt.
The Poet's Eye, in a fine Frenzy rolling,
Doth glance from Heaven to Earth, from Earth to
    Heaven;
And as Imagination bodies forth
The Forms of Things Unknown, the Poet's Pen   15
Turns them to Shapes, and gives to airy Nothing
A local Habitation and a Name.
Such Tricks hath strong Imagination
That if it would but apprehend some Joy,
It comprehends some Bringer of that Joy;   20

24 **transfigur'd** carried beyond mere figures or images to a perception of higher realms of reality. What Hippolyta refers to is the miracle by which the discords that separated the lovers have been replaced by a concord in which they are all of one mind ('Minds transfigur'd so together'). See IV.ii.4.

25 **More witnesseth than Fancy's Images** testifies to something more substantial (of greater 'Constancy', line 26) than the illusory images produced by Fancy.

27 **Admirable** to be wondered at, 'admired' in the original sense of that word, because it is mysterious or strange. Both words had much more potency in Shakespeare's time than they do in ours. *Strange* echoes line 1.

31 **Wait in** both (a) reside in, and (b) attend (serve) you in.
Boord board; table loaded with food.

32 **Masks** masques; pageants in which costumed performers combined song and dance to dramatise a theme.

39 **Abridgement** equivalent to 'interlude'; an entertainment to 'abridge' or shorten a 'torturing Hour' (line 37). Here the word *torturing* should be abridged to two syllables and pronounced 'tórch-ring'.

40 **beguile** cheat or charm away, while away. Compare I.i.239, II.i.45.

42 **Brief** short list. *Sports* echoes IV.ii.17.
ripe ready to be harvested. Compare II.ii.123–24.

44 **Battle with the Centaurs** Hercules' battle with the Centaurs (human-torsoed horses) was narrated in Book XII of Ovid's *Metamorphoses*.

Or in the Night, imagining some Fear,
How easy is a Bush suppos'd a Bear?
HIPPOLYTA   But all the Story of the Night told over,
And all their Minds transfigur'd so together,
More witnesseth than Fancy's Images,   25
And grows to something of great Constancy:
But howsoever, Strange and Admirable.

Enter Lovers: Lysander, Demetrius, Hermia, and Helena.

THESEUS   Here come the Lovers, full of Joy and
     Mirth.
Joy, gentle Friends; Joy and fresh Days of Love
Accompany your Hearts.
LYSANDER   More than to us,   30
Wait in your Royal Walks, your Boord, your Bed.
THESEUS   Come now, what Masks, what Daunces shall
     we have,
To wear away this long Age of three Hours
Between our after-Supper and Bed-time?
Where is our usual Manager of Mirth?   35
What Revels are in hand? Is there no Play
To ease the anguish of a torturing Hour?
Call Philostrate.
PHILOSTRATE   Here, mighty Theseus.
THESEUS   Say, what Abridgement have you for this
     Evening?
What Mask, what Music? How shall we beguile   40
The Lazy Time, if not with some Delight?
PHILOSTRATE   There is a Brief, how many Sports are
     ripe:
Make Choice, of which your Highness will see
     first.
THESEUS   'The Battle with the Centaurs, to be sung
By an Athenian Eunuch to the Harp'?   45
We'll none of that: that have I told my Love

48–49 **The Riot . . . Rage** The 'tipsy Bacchanals' were intoxicated women who worshipped the wine-god Bacchus and who in a mad frenzy tore 'the Thracian Singer' Orpheus to pieces; this story was told by Ovid in Book XI of the *Metamorphoses*.

50   **Devise** device; entertainment. Compare III.i.16, III.ii.35.

52   **thrice three Muses** the nine Muses, thought to preside over all the arts and sciences.

53   **Beggary** The scholar's life was proverbial for its deprivation. (See I.i.14–15.) This line is thought by some to be an oblique reference to the 1592 death of Robert Greene, a 'University Wit' who wrote plays and poems, and whose posthumous 'Groatsworth of Wit' alluded scornfully to the youthful Shakespeare as 'an upstart Crow'.

55   **sorting** both (a) consorting, keeping company with (compare III.ii.387), and (b) mixing properly. This word echoes such previous passages as III.ii.13, 21, 159, 352, and 388.

60   **Concord of this Discord** Theseus is poking fun at the oxymoronic quality of the title for the rustics' play. His words echo IV.i.112–30, 145–48. In the process they call attention to the artistry that makes *A Midsummer Night's Dream* itself so 'Strange and Admirable' in the brilliance with which it combines and transfigures such seemingly discordant components. In many ways its own form is what the 'rude Mechanicals' might call a 'lamentable Comedy' (I.ii.10–11), one that, though 'Sweet' (IV.ii.45), is at the same time an experience not unlike 'the fierce Vexation of a Dream' (IV.i.72).

64   **Tedious** This word echoes III.ii.431.

65   **fitted** Compare I.ii.66.

70   **Passion** emotional seizure.

72   **Hard-handed** with hands thick and calloused from physical labour.

74   **unbreathed** unexercised, untried in public performance.

75   **against** in preparation for. Compare I.i.124–26, III.ii.99.

76   **hear it** Plays were normally 'heard' rather than 'seen' in the Elizabethan theatre, at least by cultivated patrons, a distinction preserved in the word 'audience' (as opposed to 'spectators', the usual term for viewers at sporting events). See *Hamlet*, III.ii.44–50.

In glory of my Kinsman Hercules.
'The Riot of the tipsy Bacchanals
Tearing the Thracian Singer in their Rage'?
That is an Old Devise, and it was play'd   50
When I from Thebes came last a Conqueror.
'The thrice three Muses, mourning for the Death
Of Learning, late deceas'd in Beggary'?
That is some Satire keen and critical,
Not sorting with a Nuptial Ceremony.   55
'A tedious brief Scene of young Pyramus
And his Love Thisby; very tragical Mirth'?
Merry, and Tragical? Tedious, and Brief?
That is Hot Ice, and wondrous Strange Snow.
How shall we find the Concord of this Discord?   60
PHILOSTRATE   A Play there is, my Lord, some ten
   Words long,
Which is as Brief as I have known a Play;
But by ten Words, my Lord, it is too long,
Which makes it Tedious. For in all the Play
There is not one Word apt, one Player fitted.   65
And Tragical, my noble Lord, it is:
For Pyramus therein doth kill himself.
Which, when I saw rehears'd, I must confess,
Made mine Eyes water; but more merry Tears
The Passion of loud Laughter never shed.   70
THESEUS   What are they that do play it?
PHILOSTRATE   Hard-handed Men, that work in Athens
   here,
Which never labour'd in their Minds till now,
And now have toiled their unbreathed Memories
With this same Play against your Nuptial.   75
THESEUS   And we will hear it.
PHILOSTRATE   No, my noble Lord,
It is not for you. I have heard it over,
And it is Nothing, Nothing in the World;

79 **Sport** amusement. See line 42.

80 **stretch'd** strained to the limit.
  conn'd learned, memorised. *Pain* recalls I.i.250–51. It thereby
  reminds us of the 'cruel Pain' Helena and her friends have
  endured, and of the recompense they now enjoy for their 'dear
  Expense'.

83 **Simpleness** innocence, honesty, naïvety, artlessness. Compare
  III.ii.317.
  Duty a sense of duty and obeisance.
  tender offer, present. See III.ii.87.

85 **Wretchedness o'ercharg'd** distressed servants overtaxed or
  overworked. *O'ercharg'd* echoes *discharge* (IV.ii.8).

90 **Mistake** here used punningly as the antithesis of *Take*.
  Compare III.ii.88.

91 **Poor** inadequate, pitiable, humble.

92 **in Might, not Merit** in accordance with the quantity of the
  effort rather than the quality of the results.

93 **great Clerks** eminent scholars. *Come* means 'been'.

94 **premeditated** carefully prepared, preplanned.

95 **shiver** shake nervously.

96 **Make Periods** come to full stops.

97 **Throttle** choke off.

98 **dumbly** rendered speechless.

100 **pick'd** picked out, perceived; took.

102 **rattling** loosely flapping, as opposed to 'tongue-tied' (line 104).

104 **saucy** impudent, unruly. The slang word 'sassy' is a variant of
  'saucy'.

105 **my Capacity** my ability to make allowances because of my
  magnanimity or greatness of soul. No doubt Theseus means
  what he says. But as soon as the play begins, he and his
  companions appear to forget about such noble graciousness.

106 **address'd** ready, presented.

Unless you can find Sport in their Intents,
Extremely stretch'd, and conn'd with cruel Pain,   80
To do you Service.
THESEUS   I will hear that Play:
For never any thing can be amiss
When Simpleness and Duty tender it.
Go bring them in. – And take your places, Ladies.
HIPPOLYTA I love not to see Wretchedness
     o'ercharged,   85
And Duty in his Service perishing.
THESEUS Why, gentle Sweet, you shall see no such
     thing.
HIPPOLYTA He says they can do Nothing in this Kind.
THESEUS The Kinder we, to give them Thanks for
     Nothing.
Our Sport shall be to Take what they Mistake;   90
And what Poor Duty cannot do, Noble Respect
Takes it in Might, not Merit.
Where I have come, great Clerks have purposed
To greet me with premeditated Welcomes;
Where I have seen them shiver and look pale,   95
Make Periods in the midst of Sentences,
Throttle their practis'd Accent in their Fears,
And in Conclusion dumbly have broke off,
Not paying me a Welcome. Trust me, Sweet,
Out of this Silence yet I pick'd a Welcome;   100
And in the Modesty of fearful Duty
I read as much as from the rattling Tongue
Of saucy and audacious Eloquence.
Love, therefore, and tongue-tied Simplicity
In Least speak Most to my Capacity.   105
PHILOSTRATE So please your Grace, the Prologue is
     address'd.
DUKE Let him approach.

108– **If we offend . . . know** Quince's Prologue illustrates what
17 Theseus was saying earlier about making 'Periods in the midst
of Sentences' (line 96). Characteristically, Peter Quince *does*
'offend', and in more ways than he could conceive; but owing
to 'the Modesty of fearful Duty' (line 101), none of what he
says could ever give offence. See the note to line 118.

118 **Points** literally, punctuation. The expression *stand upon points*
carried much the same meaning as 'stand upon ceremony'
(adhere strictly to the rules of decorum). Theseus is probably
jesting only about Peter Quince's enunciation. But 'stand
upon Points' can also refer to the erection of a man's 'Good
Will', an unintended sense here reinforced by the repetition of
such words as *come* and *know*. See the notes to I.ii.10, 20, 94,
and IV.ii.4, 9, 11, 12, 21.

120 **Stop** full stop or full point ('period' in USA).

121– **speak true** both (a) speak truthfully, and (b) speak truly,
22 suitably. Lysander takes a proverb normally conveying the
first 'moral' and applies it to the second. From this point on
during the playlet, the members of the onstage audience speak
in prose, condescending to the normal discourse of the
Mechanicals and thereby heightening the ludicrousness of the
verse in the play the Mechanicals are performing.

123 **play'd** performed, as on a musical instrument.

124 **Recorder** a reed instrument, forerunner of the flute.

124– **in Government** under proper discipline or control.
25

126– **tangled Chain . . . disordered** All the links are in good
27 condition, but the relationships among them are in complete
disarray.

132 **certain** pronounced, abnormally and thus comically, with a
strong accent on the long second syllable. Like much in this
play, a good deal of the language is 'Extremely stretch'd (line
80).

134 **sunder** separate, keep apart.

Flourish of Trumpets. Enter the Prologue.

PROLOGUE   If we offend, it is with our Good Will.
That you should think, we come not to offend,
But with Good Will. To shew our simple Skill,   110
That is the true Beginning of our End.
Consider then, we come but in Despight.
We do not come, as minding to content you,
Our true Intent is. All for your Delight,
We are not here. That you should here repent
you,   115
The Actors are at hand; and, by their Show,
You shall know all, that you are like to know.
THESEUS   This Fellow doth not stand upon Points.
LYSANDER   He hath rid his Prologue, like a rough
Colt: he knows not the Stop. A good Moral, my   120
Lord: it is not enough to speak, but to speak
true.
HIPPOLYTA   Indeed he hath play'd on this Prologue,
like a Child on a Recorder, a Sound; but not in
Government.   125
THESEUS   His Speech was like a tangled Chain:
nothing impaired, but all disordered. Who is
next?

Enter Pyramus, and Thisby, and Wall, and
Moonshine, and Lion.

PROLOGUE   Gentles, perchance you wonder at this
Show.
But wonder on, till Truth make all things plain.   130
This Man is Pyramus, if you would know;
This beauteous Lady Thisby is certain.
This Man, with Lime and Roughcast, doth present
Wall, that vile Wall, which did these Lovers
sunder:

137   **Bush**   This word recalls III.ii.406.

141   **hight**   is called; an archaic verb meant to burlesque the old-fashioned dramaturgy typified by the playlet.

143   **scarre**   'Scare' is no doubt the word Quince intends, but 'scar' is amusingly pertinent too.
     affright   ludicrously redundant for 'scare away'.

144   **did fall**   let fall.

146   **Anon**   soon. *Tall* means 'valiant' here.

148–   **with Blade . . . Breast**   Shakespeare mimics the excessively
49   alliterative style of the crude older dramatic entertainments.

149   **broach'd**   breached, opened up.

152   **Lovers twain**   the two lovers.

153   **At large discourse**   speak at greater length. *Discourse* recalls IV.i.181 and IV.ii.29.

160   **crannied Hole or Chink**   This phrase is redundant, and it unintentionally calls attention to the 'Person' (IV.ii.11), the anatomy, of the actor playing Wall.

163   **Loam**   mixture of clay, sand, and straw used in plaster. One meaning of *Stone* is 'testicle' (see *Romeo and Juliet*, I.iii.53), and that raises interesting possibilities for *Loam, Roughcast,* and *Cranny*, as Theseus suggests with his reference to 'Lime and Hair' (line 167).

165   **right and sinister**   Apparently Wall is trying to indicate that the cranny is horizontal, running to the right and left ('left' is the root meaning of *sinister*). But other meanings of *right* (proper, in order) and *sinister* (ominous, suspicious) peer through Wall's cranny in comically oxymoronic ways that distract us from the straightforward information he seeks to impart. *Right* can also mean 'upright', and that sense gives *sinister* a threatening cast.

And through Wall's Chink, poor Souls, they are
    content   135
    To whisper. At the which, let no Man wonder.
This Man, with Lantern, Dog, and Bush of Thorn,
    Presenteth Moonshine. For if you will know,
By Moonshine did these Lovers think no scorn
    To meet at Ninus' Tomb, there, there to woo.   140
This grisly Beast, which Lion hight by Name,
    The trusty Thisby, coming first by Night,
Did scarre away, or rather did affright.
    And as she fled, her Mantle she did fall:
Which Lion vile with bloody Mouth did stain.   145
    Anon comes Pyramus, sweet Youth, and tall,
And finds his trusty Thisby's Mantle slain:
    Whereat, with Blade, with bloody, blameful
      Blade,
He bravely broach'd his boiling bloody Breast.
    And Thisby, tarrying in Mulberry Shade,   150
His Dagger drew, and died. For all the rest,
    Let Lion, Moonshine, Wall, and Lovers twain
At large discourse, while here they do remain.
THESEUS   I wonder, if the Lion be to speak.
DEMETRIUS   No wonder, my Lord: one Lion may, when   155
many Asses do.   *Exeunt Thisby, Lion, and Moonshine.*
WALL   In this same Interlude it doth befall
    That I, one Snout, by name, present a Wall:
    And such a Wall, as I would have you think
That had in it a crannied Hole or Chink,   160
    Through which the Lovers, Pyramus and Thisby,
    Did whisper often, very secretly.
This Loam, this Rough-cast, and this Stone doth
    show,
    That I am that same Wall: the truth is so.
And this the Cranny is, right and sinister,   165

169 **Partition** both (a) wall, and (b) division of a formal 'discourse' (from Latin *partitio*), or section of a scholarly tome. Here *wittiest* (most artful and clever) probably plays on the genital sense noted at IV.ii.9. That implication is furthered by *stand'st* in line 177.

172 **grim-look'd** grim-looking. The three lines begun here are ludicrously redundant: they reiterate the profound observation that night, after all, is night.

183 **thy Stones** In conjunction with 'thy Chink' (line 179), this phrase unintentionally calls the audience's attention to the stones of the actor playing Wall.

184 **being sensible** Theseus puns on two meanings: (a) being sentient (able to feel, as if it were a living thing), and (b) being intelligent and responsive (and thus capable of responding to an insult with a 'curse again', a reply in kind).

189 **pat** precisely.

191 **Moans** This word recalls 'hermonious' (II.i.151).

Through which the fearful Lovers are to whisper.

THESEUS   Would you desire Lime and Hair to speak
better?

DEMETRIUS   It is the wittiest Partition that ever I
heard discourse, my Lord.   170

Pyramus approaches.

THESEUS   Pyramus draws near the Wall: silence.

PYRAMUS   O grim-look'd Night, O Night with Hue so
      Black,
   O Night, which ever art, when Day is not:
   O Night, O Night, alack, alack, alack,
      I fear my Thisby's Promise is forgot.   175
   — And thou O Wall, O sweet, O lovely Wall,
      That stand'st between her Father's Ground and
         mine,
   Thou Wall, O Wall, O sweet and lovely Wall,
      Show me thy Chink, to blink through with mine
         Eyne.
   Thanks, courteous Wall; Jove shield thee well,
         for this.   180
      But what see I? No Thisby do I see.
   O wicked Wall, through whom I see no Bliss,
      Curs'd be thy Stones for thus deceiving me.

THESEUS   The Wall, me thinks, being sensible,
should curse again.   185

PYRAMUS   No in truth, Sir, he should
not: 'Deceiving me' is Thisby's Cue. She is to
enter now, and I am to spy her through the Wall.
You shall see it will fall pat as I told you:
yonder she comes.   190

Enter Thisby.

THISBY   O Wall, full often hast thou heard my Moans,

193   **cherry Lips . . . Stones**   These words elicit comically bawdy connotations totally lost on the speaker, Thisby.

194   **Knit up in thee**   intermingled with you. Thisby's phrasing echoes IV.i.184. It also hints at both erection and copulation. Compare *straight way* in line 205, *come* in line 206, and *Part discharg'd* in line 207.

196   **spy and**   see if.

198   **Grace**   gift, graciousness.

199   **Limander**   Pyramus means 'Leander' from the Greek legend about Hero and Leander, two other star-crossed lovers. But Limander, which picks up the reference to 'Lime' in line 194, provides the audience with a reminder of Lysander's similar tribulations. In similar fashion, 'Helen' (instead of Hero) in line 200 reminds us of the Helena who is in the onstage audience watching the playlet being performed. Thisby's promise to be as 'trusty' as 'Helen' (lines 199–200) is typical of the sophistication of the Mechanicals' script. Helen of Troy was proverbial for the infidelity that prompted the most famous war of Antiquity.

201   **Shafalus . . . Procrus**   Bottom's corruptions for Cephalus and Procris. In Book VII of his *Metamorphoses* Ovid describes how Cephalus mistakenly killed his wife Procris with a javelin she had given him.

203   **vild**   vile.

206   **Tide**   betide, come.

207   **discharg'd**   This word recalls IV.ii.8, and anticipates line 365.

209   **Moral down**   This phrase from the First Folio seems to be a pun on *moral* and *mural* (wall), and thus a 'witty Partition' of the Duke's (see line 169). The Quarto text, which reads 'Moon used', is difficult to make sense of, and may have resulted from an undecipherable passage in the manuscript provided to the printer.

210   **Neighbours**   Theseus' phrasing recalls Bottom's remark about peacemaking 'honest Neighbours' in III.i.144–48.

214   **Shadows**   illusions, insubstantial things. Compare III.ii.347.

215   **amend**   correct and augment, 'piece out' (*Henry V*, Prologue, 23). *Amend* recalls II.i.118, and anticipates V.ii.60, 64, 68.

For parting my fair Pyramus and me.
My cherry Lips have often kiss'd thy Stones:
  Thy Stones, with Lime and Hair knit up in thee.
PYRAMUS   I see a Voice: now will I to the Chink,   195
To spy and I can hear my Thisby's Face.
Thisby?
THISBY   My Love thou art, my Love I think.
PYRAMUS   Think what thou wilt, I am thy Lover's
  Grace;
And like Limander, am I trusty still.
THISBY   And I, like Helen, till the Fates me kill.   200
PYRAMUS   Not Shafalus to Procrus was so true.
THISBY   As Shafalus to Procrus, I to you.
PYRAMUS   O kiss me, through the Hole of this vild
  Wall.
THISBY   I kiss the Wall's Hole, not your Lips at
  all.
PYRAMUS   Wilt thou at Ninny's Tomb meet me
  straight way?   205
THISBY   Tide Life, tide Death, I come without
  Delay.   [*Exeunt Pyramus and Thisby.*]
WALL   Thus have I, Wall, my Part discharged so;
  And being done, thus Wall away doth go.   *Exit.*
DUKE   Now is the Moral down between the two
  Neighbours.   210
DEMETRIUS   No Remedy, my Lord, when Walls are so
  wilful, to hear without Warning.
DUCHESS   This is the silliest stuff that ever I
  heard.
DUKE   The Best in this Kind are but Shadows; and
  the Worst are no worse if Imagination amend them.   215
DUCHESS   It must be your Imagination, then, and not
  theirs.
DUKE   If we imagine no worse of them than they

219 **pass** (a) be admitted, (b) be accepted as sound currency, (c) pass their test. Lines 218–19 recall IV.ii.17–18.

220 **Here . . . Lion** Most editors move the Quarto's comma so that it follows *Beasts*.

226 **Lion's Dam** lion's mother; that is, a lioness.

230 **Conscience** both (a) moral sensibility, and (b) consciousness, intellect.

231 **Best at a Beast** Demetrius puns on 'bestial'.

234 **Goose for his Discretion** The goose was thought to be a silly animal; hence a goose was the antithesis of a creature with 'discretion' or intelligence. Similarly, the fox was known not for his 'Valour' but for his 'Discretion' (here, cunning, intelligence). *Discretion* echoes I.ii.80–82.

236 **carry** support; bear up and make amends for.

242 **Lanthorn** This spelling of *lantern*, introduced at this point for the first time in the Quarto, reflects the fact that lanterns were made of thin sheets of horn. The play on *horned* leads to the joke that the Man in the Moon is a cuckold, traditionally represented as a man with horns on his forehead (line 243).

244– **He is no Crescent . . . Circumference** Theseus' comment is
45 based on the fact that the Man in the Moon was normally represented as a crescent, whereas here 'the Circumference' (that is, the full Moon) makes the Man in the Moon's horns (the points of the Moon's crescent) 'invisible'.

of themselves, they may pass for Excellent Men.
Here come two Noble Beasts, in a Man and a Lion.   220

Enter Lion and Moonshine.

LION   You Ladies, you (whose gentle Hearts do fear
    The smallest monstrous Mouse that creeps on
      Floor),
    May now, perchance, both quake and tremble here,
      When Lion rough, in wildest Rage, doth roar.
    Then know that I, as Snug the Joiner, am   225
      A Lion fell, nor else no Lion's Dam.
    For if I should, as Lion, come in strife,
      Into this Place, 'twere pity on my Life.
DUKE   A very gentle Beast, and of a good
Conscience.   230
DEMETRIUS   The very Best at a Beast, my Lord, that
e'er I saw.
LYSANDER   This Lion is a very Fox, for his Valour.
DUKE   True: and a Goose for his Discretion.
DEMETRIUS   Not so, my Lord. For his Valour cannot   235
carry his Discretion; and the Fox carries the
Goose.
DUKE   His Discretion, I am sure, cannot carry
his Valour: for the Goose carries not the Fox. It
is well: leave it to his Discretion, and let us   240
listen to the Moon.
MOON   This Lanthorn doth the Horned Moon present.
DEMETRIUS   He should have worn the Horns, on his
Head.
DUKE   He is no Crescent, and his Horns are
invisible, within the Circumference.   245
MOON   This Lanthorn doth the Horned Moon present;
My self the Man i'th' Moon, do seem to be.
DUKE   This is the greatest Error of all the rest:

251– **He dares . . . Snuff** Demetrius says that the actor playing Moon
52   is afraid to put himself into the lantern because of the candle,
    which is already in danger of being 'snuffed out'.

254 **change** Hippolyta's wish for a 'change' in the phase of the
    Moon (here an impatient desire to see the actor playing Moon
    move on) echoes Theseus' opening lines of the play (I.i.3–6);
    it thus serves as yet another way of bringing the action back
    full circle.

259– **All that I have to say . . . Dog my Dog** Having had his
61   prepared speech interrupted twice by the irreverent comments
    of the courtly audience, Flute now resigns himself to
    paraphrasing his lines in prose.

260 **i'th'** in the. The phrase had become so common that *in the* was
    contracted into the one-syllable *i'th'*.

266 **Oh** This word represents the Lion's roar.

271 **Well mouz'd** well moused (that is, picked up and shaken as if
    the mantle were a mouse).

273 **And . . . vanished** Most editors assume tht Lion exits here. But
    in the version of the script preserved in the First Quarto he
    needs to remain visible to the audience so that he can speak
    lines 355–58. Most editors follow the Folio and assign those
    lines to Bottom. But the playwright may (initially at least)
    have wanted to give Snug a chance to extemporise (see
    I.ii.67–70).

274 **Sunny Beams** Typically, Bottom attributes Sun-like
    luminescence to the Moon.

the Man should be put into the Lanthorn. How is
it else the Man i'th' Moon?   250
DEMETRIUS   He dares not come there for the Candle:
for you see, it is already in Snuff.
DUCHESS   I am aweary of this Moon. Would he would
change.
DUKE   It appears, by his small Light of Discretion,   255
than he is in the Wane; but yet in Courtesy, in
all Reason, we must stay the Time.
LYSANDER   Proceed, Moon.
MOON   All that I have to say, is to tell you, that the
Lanthorn is the Moon, I the Man i'th' Moon, this   260
Thornbush my Thornbush, and this Dog my Dog.
DEMETRIUS   Why, all these should be in the Lanthorn;
for all these are in the Moon. But silence: here
comes Thisby.

Enter Thisby.

THISBY   This is old Ninny's Tomb. Where is my Love?   265
LION   Oh.

The Lion roars, Thisby runs off.

DEMETRIUS   Well roar'd, Lion.
DUKE   Well run, Thisby.
DUCHESS   Well shone, Moon. – Truly, the Moon shines
with a good Grace.   270
DUKE   Well mouz'd, Lion.

Enter Pyramus.

DEMETRIUS   And then came Pyramus.
LYSANDER   And so the Lion vanish'd.
PYRAMUS   Sweet Moon, I thank thee, for thy Sunny
Beams;

286 **Furies fell** angry Furies. The Furies were avenging spirits, usually in threes (Tisiphone, Megaera, and Alecto), who were sent from Tartarus (the abyss below Hades) to punish crimes.

287– **O Fates . . . Thrum** The Fates were three goddesses, one of
88 whom (Clotho) was said to spin, another (Lachesis) to draw, and a third (Atropos) to cut the thread of human life. The *thrum* is the tufted end of the thread fastened to the loom.

289 **Quail** overwhelm.
quell kill.

292 **Beshrew** curse. Compare II.ii.60.

293 **wherefore** why.

294 **deflour'd** deflowered; violated sexually.

299 **Pap** nipple, teat. At some point – probably at several points (line 302) – during this speech Pyramus stabs himself.

306 **loose** both (a) loose, let go, and (b) lose.

I thank thee, Moon, for shining now so bright.   275
For by thy gracious, golden, glittering Beams
    I trust to take of truest Thisby sight.
        But stay: O spight!
        But mark, poor Knight,
What dreadful Dole is here?   280
        Eyes, do you see!
        How can it be?
O dainty Duck, O Dear!
        Thy Mantle good,
        What, stain'd with Blood?   285
Approach, ye Furies fell;
        O Fates come, come,
        Cut Thread and Thrum;
Quail, crush, conclude, and quell.

DUKE   This Passion, and the Death of a dear   290
    Friend, would go near to make a Man look sad.

DUCHESS   Beshrew my Heart, but I pity the Man.

PYRAMUS   O wherefore, Nature, didst thou Lions
        frame?
    Since Lion vild hath here deflour'd my Dear?
Which is – no, no, which was – the fairest Dame   295
    That liv'd, that lov'd, that lik'd, that look'd
        with Cheer.
        Come, Tears, confound;
        Out, Sword, and wound
    The Pap of Pyramus:
        Ay, that left Pap,   300
        Where Heart doth hop.
Thus die I, thus, thus, thus.
        Now am I dead,
        Now am I fled,
My Soul is in the Sky.   305
        Tongue, loose thy Light,
        Moon, take thy Flight;   [*Exit Moonshine.*]
Now die, die, die, die, die.

309– **No Die . . . but One** Demetrius says that rather than a full die
10 (that is, one of a pair of dice) with six faces, Pyramus is only
the face with a single spot (the ace).

311 **Less than an Ace** Lysander replies that Pyramus is actually
even less than one now. *Nothing* recalls line 16 and
IV.ii.13–14. Lysander appears to be picking up on the erotic
sense of *die* (achieve orgasm); if so, his point is that Bottom is
no longer an erect 1 but a wilted o. Lines 313–16 suggest that
Thisby can provide the surgery that will 'recover' him.

314 **yet prove an Ass** Theseus puns on *ace/ass*, but in doing so he
also unknowingly alludes to Bottom's earlier 'translation' into
a real ass.

318 **Passion** grief. Compare lines 69–70.

321 **Moth** alternate spelling for *mote*, a speck (most familiar to us
now from Matthew 7:3 and Luke 6:41 in the King James
Bible). See the note to III.i.163.
Balance balance scales. Compare III.ii.130–33.

323 **warnd** either (a) warned, or (b) warrant (shield). The Quarto
spelling is reproduced here without alteration.

327 **videlicet** that is, namely.

330 **arise** In view of the wordplay in lines 309–16, this verb hints at
more than one kind of 'Passion' (line 318). Compare line 348,
which parodies the heroine's erotically charged death in
V.iii.171–72 of *Romeo and Juliet*. Theseus alludes to the inept
suggestiveness of Thisby's 'death' in lines 362–64; *hang'd
himself* could refer either to copulation (as in *Measure for
Measure*, IV.ii.33–43) or to masturbation (as in *Love's
Labour's Lost*, V.ii.588–600).

331 **dumbe** dumb, incapable of speech. Here the Quarto spellings
are retained, to preserve the special character of this rhyme.

340 **Sisters Three** the Fates.

DEMETRIUS   No Die, but an Ace for him; for he is
but One.   310
LYSANDER   Less than an Ace, Man: for he is Dead, he
is Nothing.
DUKE   With the help of a Surgeon he might yet
recover, and yet prove an Ass.
DUCHESS   How chance Moonshine is gone before?   315
Thisby comes back and finds her Lover.
DUKE   She will find him by Star-light.

Enter Thisby.

Here she comes, and her Passion ends the Play.
DUCHESS   Me thinks she should not use a long one
for such a Pyramus: I hope she will be brief.   320
DEMETRIUS   A Moth will turn the Balance which
Pyramus, which Thisby, is the better: he for a
Man, God warnd us, she for a Woman, God bless
us.
LYSANDER   She hath spied him already with those   325
sweet Eyes.
DEMETRIUS   And thus she means, *videlicet.*
THISBY   Asleep, my Love?
        What, dead, my Dove?
    O Pyramus arise;   330
        Speak, speak. Quite dumbe?
        Dead, dead? A Tumbe
    Must cover thy sweet Eyes.
        These lily Lips,
        This cherry Nose,   335
    These yellow cowslip Cheeks,
        Are gone, are gone:
        Lovers, make moan.
    His Eyes were green as Leeks.
        O Sisters Three,   340
        Come, come to me

343 **Gore** blood.

344 **shore** shorn, cut.

348 **imbrew** both (a) soak with blood, and (b) brew, embroil. As she speaks her final words, Thisby raises her blade and stabs herself. Compare line 149.

355– **the Wall is down that parted their Fathers** The feud between
56 the families of the lovers in *Romeo and Juliet*, a play probably written around the same time as *A Midsummer Night's Dream*, functions as a symbolic wall, and one that is finally brought down only with the deaths of the hero and heroine. In the Folio, lines 355–58 are assigned to Bottom. Like many of the other alterations in the Folio version of the play (see the note to IV.i.182), that change probably reflects a different set of performance conditions.

359– **No Epilogue . . . no Excuse** As Puck's concluding speech
60 illustrates (lines 427–42), an epilogue was normally intended to provide an apology for the inadequacies of the dramatic fictions or 'Shadows' (line 214) just presented.

364 **fine** superb. But Theseus may also be punning on *fine* as a variant of *finis* (end), to suggest that it would have been, in at least one sense, a finished tragedy. Compare line 12, and see IV.i.85.

366 **Bergomask** a rustic dance apparently associated with the Bergamo region of northern Italy.

367 **iron Tongue** the bell clapper.
told a play on 'tolled', continuing the 'Tongue' metaphor.

371 **palpable gross** crudely literal in its physicality. *Beguil'd* recalls line 40.

372 **Gate** Theseus probably means *gait* (the two words are not usually distinguishable by spelling in Shakespeare, but *Gate* could fit the context too. This spelling occurs in both the Quarto and the Folio.

373 **hold** maintain.
Solemnity festival season.

With Hands as pale as Milk;
  Lay them in Gore,
  Since you have shore
With Shears his Threed of Silk.   345
  Tongue, not a Word:
  Come, trusty Sword,
Come Blade, my Breast imbrew:
  And farewell, Friends:
  Thus Thisby ends.   350
Adieu, adieu, adieu.

DUKE   Moonshine and Lion are left to bury the
  Dead.

DEMETRIUS   Ay, and Wall too.

LION   No, I assure you: the Wall   355
  is down, that parted their Fathers. Will it
  please you to see the Epilogue, or to hear a
  Bergomask daunce between two of our Company?

DUKE   No Epilogue, I pray you: for your Play
  needs no Excuse. Never excuse: for when the   360
  Players are all dead, there need none to be
  blam'd. Mary, if he that writ it had play'd
  Pyramus, and hang'd himself in Thisby's Garter,
  it would have been a fine Tragedy. And so it is,
  truly, and very notably discharg'd. But come   365
  your Bergomask; let your Epilogue alone.
    The iron Tongue of Midnight hath told Twelve:
    Lovers to Bed, 'tis almost Fairy Time.
    I fear we shall outsleep the coming Morn
    As much as we this Night have overwatch'd.   370
    This palpable gross Play hath well beguil'd
    The heavy Gate of Night. Sweet Friends, to Bed.
    A Fortnight hold we this Solemnity,
    In nightly Revels and new Jollity.   *Exeunt.*

V.ii   Modern editions usually treat the Fairies' 'epilogue' as the conclusion of V.i. But the stage is cleared with the *Exeunt* at V.i.374 (a vacated stage being the standard criterion for a scene change), and normal practice thus calls for a new scene designation. The Quarto has no act or scene divisions; the Folio divides this play into acts only (in contrast with its usual procedure of segmenting plays into both acts and scenes).

2   **beholds**   observes. Most editors emend to *behowls*; but since this idea is implicit in the manner of 'beholding' associated with wolves, no alteration in the text is necessary. Puck's phrasing harks back to I.i.7–11.

4   **fordoone**   completely done. The Quarto spelling, here retained, shows that this word is meant to rime with *Moon*.

5   **wasted Brands**   dying embers.

6   **Screech-Owl**   thought to be a bird of ill omen, whose cry foretold death.

8   **In remembrance of a Shroud**   in mind of a burial cloth. Lines 383–86 recall III.ii.378–95.

14   **Triple Hecate's Team**   the horses carrying the Goddess of the Moon from the Sun's presence. Hecate had three aspects or personae in her rule over the realms of Hades (where she was known as Persephone), Earth (Diana), and the Heavens (Cynthia or Phoebe).

17   **frolic**   at play.

18   **hallowed**   made holy, consecrated.

22   **Fier**   fire; so spelled in the Quarto to rhyme with *Brier*.

27   **by rote**   according to ritual; by memory or habit.

Scene 2

Enter Puck.

PUCK   Now the hungry Lion roars,
    And the Wolf beholds the Moon;
Whilst the heavy Ploughman snores,
    All with weary Tasks fordoone.
Now the wasted Brand do glow   5
    Whilst the Screech-Owl, screeching loud,
Puts the Wretch that lies in Woe
    In remembrance of a Shroud.
Now is the Time of Night
    That the Graves, all gaping wide,   10
Every one lets forth his Spright,
    In the Churchway Paths to glide.
And we Fairies, that do run
    By the Triple Hecate's Team
From the presence of the Sun,   15
    Following Darkness like a Dream,
Now are frolic. Not a Mouse
Shall disturb this hallowed House.
I am sent, with Broom, before,
To sweep the Dust behind the Door.   20

Enter the King and Queen of Fairies, with all their Train.

OBERON   Through the House give glimmering Light,
    By the dead and drowsy Fier;
Every Elf and Fairy Spright,
    Hop as light as Bird from Brier,
And this Ditty after me   25
    Sing and daunce it trippingly.
TITANIA   First rehearse your Song by rote,
    To each Word a warbling Note.
Hand in Hand, with Fairy Grace,
    Will we sing and bless this Place.   30
OBERON   Now until the break of Day

35 **Issue there create** offspring there conceived.

42 **Mark Prodigious** birthmark indicating a prodigy, or child set off from birth as in some way abnormal (here in a negative way).

43 **Nativity** birth.

45 **consecrate** consecrated, made sacred.

46 **Gate** As in V.i.372, either 'gait' or 'gate' could fit the context.

47 **several** separate.

453 **Shadows** Here Shakespeare means both (a) Fairies, unseen or imaginary creatures, and (b) actors, products of the poet's imagination. Compare V.i.214.

56 **Visions** In this context, Puck means (a) dreams, (b) special insights or revelations, and (c) the entire play.

57 **Theme** dramatic action.

58 **No more yielding but a Dream** yielding to rational analysis no more than a dream does, or having no more substance than a dream has.

59 **reprehend** blame, hold to account.

62 **unearned Luck** more luck than we deserve.

63 **Serpent's Tongue** the hisses of the snake. Here Puck draws a parallel with the sounds made by a disapproving audience; he also alludes to one of the names associated with the Devil, who assumed the form of a serpent and spoke to Eve with a forked tongue in the Garden of Eden (Genesis 3).

64 **Amends** restitution, corrections. Puck's noun echoes line 215.

Through this House each Fairy stray.
To the best Bride-Bed will we,
Which by us shall blessed be;
And the Issue there create   35
Ever shall be fortunate;
So shall all the Couples three
Ever true in Loving be;
And the Blots of Nature's Hand
Shall not in their Issue stand.   40
Never Mole, Harelip, nor Scar,
Nor Mark Prodigious, such as are
Despised in Nativity,
Shall upon their Children be.
With this Field-dew consecrate,   45
Every Fairy take his Gate,
And each several Chamber bless
Through this Palace with sweet Peace.
And the Owner of it bless'd
Ever shall in Safety rest.   50
Trip away; make no Stay;
Meet me all by break of Day.

                                Exeunt [all but Puck.]

PUCK   If we Shadows have offended,
Think but this, and all is mended:
That you have but slumb'red here   55
While these Visions did appear;
And this weak and idle Theme,
No more yielding but a Dream,
Gentles, do not reprehend.
If you pardon, we will mend.   60
And as I am an honest Puck,
If we have unearned Luck
Now to scape the Serpent's Tongue,
We will make Amends ere long,
Else the Puck a Liar call.   65
So good night unto you all.

68   **Give me your Hands**   applaud by clapping, and thereby extend
        to us your fellowship as friends.

Give me your Hands if we be Friends,
And Robin shall restore Amends.

FINIS

PERSPECTIVES ON
A Midsummer Night's Dream

On 29 September 1662 Samuel Pepys recorded in his diary that he had just seen a performance of *A Midsummer Night's Dream*. It was, he said, a play he 'had never seen before, nor shall ever again, for it is the most insipid ridiculous play that ever I saw in my life'.

A century later, in the preface to his 1765 edition of the dramatist's complete works, Samuel Johnson was somewhat kinder to the comedy, but he could not forbear wondering 'how Shakespear, who commonly derived his knowledge of nature from his own observation, happened to place the glow-worm's light in his eyes, which is only in his tail'. Johnson also found it odd that the dramatist decided to call the work 'a *Midsummer-Night's Dream*, when he so carefully informs us that it happened on the night preceding May day'. On the other hand, Johnson conceded (as he put it in the notes to his 1773 edition) that

> Wild and fantastical as this play is, all the parts in their various modes are well written and give the kind of pleasure which the author designed. Fairies in his time were much in fashion; common tradition had made them familiar, and [Edmund] Spenser's poem [*The Faerie Queene*] had made them great.

What seems to have engaged Johnson's attention more than anything else in *A Midsummer Night's Dream* was the way the scenes involving the 'rude Mechanicals' show the author taking

advantage of his knowledge of the theatre to ridicule the prejudices
and competitions of the players. Bottom, who is generally acknow-
ledged the principal actor, declares his inclination to be for a tyrant,
for a party of fury, tumult, and noise, such as every young man pants
to perform when he first steps upon the stage. The same Bottom, who
seems bred in a tiring room, has another histrionic passion. He is for
engrossing every part and would exclude his inferiors from all
possibility of distinction. He is therefore desirous to play Pyramus,
Thisbe, and the Lion at the same time. . . . In the time of Shakespear
there were many companies of players, sometimes five at the same
time, contending for the favour of the public. Of these some were
undoubtedly very unskilful and very poor, and it is probable that the
[playwright's] design . . . was to ridicule their ignorance, and the odd
expedients to which they might be driven by want of proper
decorations. Bottom was perhaps the head of a rival house, and is
therefore honoured with an Ass's head.

William Hazlitt (*The Characters of Shakespear's Plays*, London, 1818) also found the Mechanicals of interest, but for
different reasons.

Bottom the Weaver is a character that has not had justice done him.
He is the most romantic of mechanics. And what a list of companions
he has – Quince the Carpenter, Snug the Joiner, Flute the Bellows
Mender, Snout the Tinker, Starveling the Tailor; and then again, what
a group of fairy attendants, Puck, Peaseblossom, Cobweb, Moth, and
Mustardseed! It has been observed that Shakespear's characters are
constructed upon deep physiological principles; and there is something in this play which looks very like it. Bottom the Weaver . . .
follows a sedentary trade, and he is accordingly represented as
conceited, serious, and fantastical. He is ready to undertake anything
and everything, as if it was as much a matter of course as the motion of
his loom and shuttle. . . . Snug the Joiner is the moral man of the piece,
who proceeds by measurement and discretion in all things. You see
him with his rule and compasses in his hand. . . .

For Hazlitt, however, the Fairies were even more remarkable than
the Mechanicals.

How beautifully is this race of beings contrasted with the men and
women actors in the scene, by a single epithet which Titania gives to
the latter, 'the human mortals'! It is astonishing that Shakespear
should be considered, not only by foreigners, but by many of our own
critics, as a gloomy and heavy writer, who painted nothing but

'gorgons and hydras, and chimeras dire.' His subtlety exceeds that of all other dramatic writers, insomuch that a celebrated person of the present day [Samuel Taylor Coleridge] said that he regarded him rather as a metaphysician than a poet. His delicacy and sportive gaiety are infinite. . . .

Unfortunately for Hazlitt, there were no productions in his day that could do justice to the artistry of *A Midsummer Night's Dream*.

> Poetry and the stage do not agree well together. The attempt to reconcile them in this instance fails not only of effect, but of decorum. The *ideal* can have no place upon the stage, which is a picture without perspective; everything there is in the foreground. That which was merely an airy shape, a dream, a passing thought, immediately becomes an unmanageable reality. Where all is left to the imagination (as is the case in reading) every circumstance, near or remote, has an equal chance of being kept in mind, and tells according to the mixed impression of all that has been suggested. . . . Thus Bottom's head in the play is a fantastic illusion, produced by magic spells: on the stage it is an ass's head, and nothing more. . . . When ghosts appear at midday, when apparitions stalk along Cheapside, then may the *Midsummer Night's Dream* be represented without injury at Covent Garden or Drury Lane. The boards of a theatre and the regions of fancy are not the same thing.

Two decades after Hazlitt praised *A Midsummer Night's Dream* for its capacity to extend our imaginations by eluding their grasp, Henry Hallam tried to explain the play's effects, in part, by noting the kinds of 'learning' it exemplified. In *Literature of Europe* (London, 1839) Hallam ventured the suggestion that Shakespeare

> possessed rather more acquaintance with the Latin language than many believe. The phrases, unintelligible and improper, except in the sense of their primitive roots, which occur so copiously in his plays, seem to be unaccountable on the supposition of absolute ignorance. In the *Midsummer Night's Dream* these are much less frequent than in his later dramas. But here we find several instances. Thus, 'things base and vile, holding no *quantity*', for value; rivers, that 'have overborne their *continents*', the *continente ripa* of Horace; '*compact* of imagination', 'something of great *constancy*', for consistency; 'sweet Pyramus *translated* there'; the law of Athens, 'which by no means we may

extenuate'. I have considerable doubts whether any of these expressions would be found in the contemporary prose of Elizabeth's reign,
which was less overrun by pedantry than that of her successor; but,
could authority be produced for Latinisms so forced, it is still not
likely that one, who did not understand their proper meaning, would
have introduced them into poetry.

Later in the century, in *Shakspere: A Critical Study of His Mind
and Art* (3rd edn, London, 1877), Edward Dowden, alluding to
the theory that the play 'was written on the occasion of some
noble couple, possibly for the marriage of the poet's patron
Southampton with Elizabeth Vernon', argued that

> The central figure of the play is that of Theseus. There is no figure in
> the early drama of Shakspere so magnificent. His are the large hands
> that have helped to shape the world. His utterance is the rich-toned
> speech of one who is master of events – who has never known a shrill
> or eager feeling. His nuptial day is at hand; and while the other lovers
> are agitated, bewildered, incensed, Theseus, who does not think of
> himself as a lover, but rather as a beneficent conqueror, remains in
> calm possession of his joy. . . . With a splendid capacity for enjoy-
> ment, gracious to all, ennobled by the glory, implied rather than
> explicit, of great foregone achievement, he stands as centre of the
> poem, giving their true proportions to the fairy tribe, upon the one
> hand, and, upon the other, to the 'human mortals.'

Turning to other aspects of the play, Dowden said that

> Comments by Shakspere upon his own art are not so numerous that
> we can afford to overlook them. It must here be noted that Shakspere
> makes the 'palpable gross' interlude of the Athenian mechanicals
> serve as an indirect apology for his own necessarily imperfect attempt
> to represent fairy land and the majestic world of heroic life. . . . [But
> to] Theseus, the great man of action, the worst and the best of these
> shadowy representations are all one. He graciously lends himself to be
> amused, and will not give unmannerly rebuff to the painstaking
> craftsmen who have so laboriously done their best to please him. . . .
> For the method of Bottom and his company is precisely the reverse, as
> Gervinus has observed, of Shakspere's own method. They are
> determined to leave nothing to be supplied by the imagination. . . .
> Shakspere as much as says, 'If you do not approve my dramatic
> method of presenting fairy land and the heroic world, here is a
> specimen of the rival method. You think my fairy world might be
> amended. Well, amend it with your own imagination. I can do no

more unless I adopt the artistic ideas of these Athenian hand-icraftsmen.'

For virtually all of the eighteenth century and for the first half of the nineteenth, the text that Shakespeare had written for *A Midsummer Night's Dream* was largely supplanted by music, dance, and other special effects. But even after something approximating the full script had been restored to stage performances, there were still things producers could try in misguided attempts to 'amend' the imaginations of audiences attending productions of the comedy. In an 1885 column in the *Saturday Review* George Bernard Shaw enumerated the excesses of one such producer. Describing Augustine Daly as a theatre manager 'in great form', Shaw said:

> In my last article I was rash enough to hint that [Daly] had not quite realized what could be done with electric lighting on the stage. He triumphantly answers me by fitting up all his fairies with portable batteries and incandescent lights, which they switch on and off from time to time, like children with a new toy. . . . Another stroke of his is to make Oberon a woman. It must not be supposed that he does this solely because it is wrong, though there is no other reason apparent. He does it partly because he was brought up to do such things, and partly because they seem to him to be a tribute to Shakespeare's greatness, which, being uncommon, ought not to be interpreted according to the dictates of common sense. . . . He swings Puck away on a clumsy trapeze with a ridiculous clash of the cymbals in the orchestra, in the fullest belief that he is thereby completing instead of destroying the effect of Puck's lines. His 'panoramic illusion of the passage of Theseus's barge to Athens' is more absurd than anything that occurs in the tragedy of Pyramus and Thisbe in the last act. . . . Theseus has to enter from his barge down a bank, picking his way through the sleeping Lysander and Hermia, Demetrius and Helena. The four lions in Trafalgar Square are not more conspicuous and unoverlookable than these four figures are. Yet Theseus has to make all his hunting speeches in an impossible unconsciousness of them, and then to look at them amazedly and exclaim, 'But soft, what nymphs are these?' as if he could in any extremity of absence of mind have missed seeing them all along.

A few years later (in a 1904 issue of *Good Words*), G. K. Chesterton offered the opinion that

The greatest of Shakespeare's comedies is also, from a certain point of view, the greatest of his plays. No one would maintain that [*A Midsummer Night's Dream*] occupied this position in the matter of psychological study, if by psychological study we mean the study of individual characters in a play. . . . But there is a sense in which the play is perhaps a greater triumph of psychology than *Hamlet* itself. . . . It is a trite matter, of course, though in a general criticism a more or less indispensable one, to comment upon . . . the extraordinarily human and accurate manner in which the play catches the atmosphere of a dream. The chase and tangle and frustration of the incidents and personalities are well known to everyone who has dreamt of perpetually falling over precipices or perpetually missing trains. While following out clearly and legally the necessary narrative of the drama, the author contrives to include every one of the main peculiarities of the exasperating dream. . . . A dream can commonly be described as possessing an utter discordance of incident combined with a curious unity of mood; everything changes but the dreamer. It may begin with anything, but if the dreamer is sad at the end he will be sad as if by prescience at the beginning; if he is cheerful at the beginning he will be cheerful if the stars fall. *A Midsummer Night's Dream* has in a most singular degree effected this difficult, this almost desperate subtlety.

If Chesterton likened the form of Shakespeare's play to that of a dream, a later observer proposed another analogy. In her book *The Court Masque: A Study in the Relationship between Poetry and Revels* (London, 1927), Enid Welsford said that

To compare a very great with a very small thing, the imaginative effect of this kind of plot weaving is like that of the transformation scenes in ballet or pantomime, where groups of dancers come in like waves of colour, melting one into another. The effect is attractive even when crudely and unbeautifully designed. Transmuted into poetry, it is of surpassing charm. It could only have been so transmuted at a time when pageantry was part of the people's life, when beauty was an element in all their recreations and 'they drew it in as simply as their breath.'

Music in the court masque was even more important than scenery. Again and again, in the accounts of Elizabethan and Jacobean revels, we are told of the entrancing quality of the music. . . . This music Shakespeare has transmuted into his poetry, as he has transmuted the spectacular element of pageantry. . . .

The rhythm of the poetry is a dance rhythm, the lines rock and sway with the movement of the fairies. Even more closely in the last scene does the verse echo the light pattering steps of the elves. . . . The plot is a pattern, a figure, rather than a series of events occasioned by human character and passion, and this pattern, especially in the moonlit parts of the play, is the pattern of a dance. . . . The appearance and reappearance of the various lovers, the will-o'-the-wisp movement of the elusive Puck, form a kind of figure ballet. The lovers quarrel in a dance pattern: first, there are two men to one woman and the other woman alone, then for a brief space a circular movement, each one pursuing and pursued, then a return to the first figure with the position of the women reversed, then a cross-movement, man quarrelling with man and woman with woman, and then, as finale, a general setting to partners, including not only lovers but fairies and royal personages as well.

But what about the Fairies? Were these sprightly creatures around before *A Midsummer Night's Dream* made them familiar to us? In *The Shakespearian Tempest* (New York, 1932) Minor White Latham pointed out that

There is ample evidence of the belief in the reality and actual being of the fairies . . . in the recognition by English law, and more especially by Scottish law, of mortals made witches by fairies who appeared to them and invested them with their powers. . . . On first acquaintance, there seems but little difference between the fairies of *A Midsummer Night's Dream* and those of native tradition. . . . On closer study, however, the fairies [in Shakespeare's play] are seen to be what Oberon calls them, 'spirits of another sort'. Whatever is homely or substantial or dangerous has been removed from the picture of them, which Shakespeare repaints, and only their rulers still invested with formidable powers and uncertain tempers. . . .

Oberon . . . seems to have been taken by Shakespeare directly from *Huon of Bordeaux*. With his quick and violent temper, his piety, his devotion to those mortals to whom he took a fancy, his angelic visage, his dwarfed stature, his splendid dress and his powers of enchantment – all characteristics of Oberon, the 'dwarfe kynge of the fayrey' in the romance – he was admirably adapted to play one of the leading parts in the imaginary and poetic fairy kingdom of a romantic comedy.

The name *Titania* Shakespeare appears to have taken from Ovid's *Metamorphoses*, where it occurs as one of the synonyms of Diana. . . .

The powers which were attributed to Diana and to Oberon, both in their own persons and in that of the king and queen of the fairies, are still exercised by the fairy rulers of Shakespeare. Their connection with mortals, however, is revealed as unfailingly beneficent and altruistic, an attitude vastly different from that of Diana, 'the goddesse of the Pagans', associated with witches in *The Discovery of Witchcraft*, and from the Oberon of whom Gerames and Huon stood in much fear in *Huon of Bordeaux*.

For the first time the fairies themselves are made consistently good. No longer do they function as the mischievous and dangerous beings they were believed to be, with occasional and erratic lapses into beneficence and the bestowal of good fortune; instead they become, in actuality, the Good Neighbours which, in flattery and fear, they had been dubbed by mortals trembling before the idea of their advent. . . .

Even the changeling in the fairy kingdom . . . has not been obtained by violence and human woe. He has been adopted by Titania out of friendship for his mother, who 'being mortal, of that boy did die'.

If *A Midsummer Night's Dream* transformed the way people thought about the traditional fairy kingdom, it also altered the way they thought about Robin Goodfellow, the 'Hobgoblin' or 'Puck' of the play. Robin's 'figure and person, if nothing else, would have marked him as a country spirit', Latham says, 'or would have kept him one. He was both tall and broad, of the size of a full grown man or bigger with nothing ethereal or graceful about his proportions. His bigness particularly set him apart from other terrestrial spirits', and had it not been for Shakespeare such a being would probably never have been thought of as related to the other fairy spirits we now recognize from *A Midsummer Night's Dream*.

Ernest Schanzer extended Latham's observations in an article on 'The Moon and the Fairies in *A Midsummer Night's Dream*' (*University of Toronto Quarterly*, 1955).

In this play we are given three wholly distinct kinds of fairies, provided we can speak of Puck as a fairy at all. He was not considered so in popular superstition, but was thought of as a spirit of another sort, whose merry pranks made him the most popular of all the sprites that haunted the English countryside.

The fairies that attend upon Titania, meanwhile, 'are conscientious and very much overworked servants of the queen, with little time for idle gossiping'. They do errands for an 'exacting mistress', and once she takes Bottom as her Prince Consort they serve him as they would their Queen.

> The Titania who winds Bottom in her arms is clearly a full-grown woman. Not only would it be unactable to have a tiny Titania make love to Bottom, but it would also be unthinkable. For the humour of their love-scenes depends on our realisation that it is a supremely beautiful woman who is enamoured of this weaver turned ass. . . . Shakespeare clearly thinks of Titania and Oberon as of the same stature as the traditional English fairies, who were considered to be of normal height or slightly below it. . .
>
> Shakespeare has been sometimes reproached with having gelded the English fairy, having robbed it of its fearfulness and hence its reality, and turned it into a trifle light as air, the mere plaything of the imagination. We can see why he should have done so for the purposes of this play. He probably felt that the traditional English fairy was too uncanny and fearful a creature to be accommodated in this scene of tragical mirth. And so, in creating the attendant fairies in this play, Shakespeare drew on a *jeu d'esprit*, written probably a few months earlier, Mercutio's Queen Mab speech.

For Paul A. Olson ('*A Midsummer Night's Dream* and the Meaning of Court Marriage', *ELH: A Journal of English Literary History*, 1957), the Fairies in Shakespeare's comedy were best viewed as relating to a world where

> Wedlock fulfilled its part in the concord of things when the male ruled his mate in the same way that reason was ordained to control both will and passions. It was argued that, before the Fall, men propagated their kind according to the promptings of charity. But with the first temptation, Eve's sensuality overcame Adam, and Adam's reason. The fall transformed all divine, rational love in man into unreasonable and selfish lust. In Bottom's words, 'Reason and Love keep little company together.' . . .
>
> In this tradition, Shakespeare's king of Shadows is . . . a delicate figure for grace. He is the play's Prospero. Like Theseus, he may have wandered in the mazes of love and war, but, again like Theseus, he has overcome these. When properly sovereign, Oberon furthers the celestial love which preserves chaste marriages and keeps the cosmos in order. His relation to the higher love is clarified in a late scene. There Puck points to the damned spirits who deliberately exiled themselves 'from night, / And must for aye consort with black browed night.' Oberon immediately objects that he is not the same sort of spirit. By reminding Puck that he has often sported with the morning's

love, he introduces an image which has behind it an accumulated tradition of reference to the sun of God's charity.

C. L. Barber took a less solemn view of the Fairies. In *Shakespeare's Festive Comedy* (Princeton, 1959), he observed that 'In making Oberon, prince of fairies, into the May king, Shakespeare urbanely plays with the notion of a supernatural power at work in holiday: he presents the common May game presided over by an aristocratic garden god.' As Barber assesses it,

> The humor of the play relates superstition, magic and passionate delusion as 'fancy's images'. The actual title emphasizes a skeptical attitude by calling the comedy a 'dream'. It seems unlikely that the title's characterization of the dream, 'a midsummer night's dream', implies association with the specific customs of Midsummer Eve, except as 'midsummer night' would carry suggestions of a magic time. The observance of Midsummer Eve in England centered on building bonfires or 'bonefires', of which there is nothing in Shakespeare's moonlight play. It was a time when maids might find out who their true love would be by dreams or divinations. There were customs of decking houses with greenery and hanging lights, which just possibly might connect with the fairies' torches at the comedy's end. . . . In the absence of evidence, there is no way to settle just how much comes from tradition. But what is clear is that Shakespeare was not *simply* writing out folklore which he heard in his youth, as Romantic critics liked to assume. On the contrary, his fairies are produced by a complex fusion of pageantry and popular game, as well as popular fancy. Moreover, . . . they are not serious in the menacing way in which the people's fairies were serious. Instead they are serious in a very different way, as embodiments of the May-game experience of eros in men and women and trees and flowers, while any superstitious tendency to believe in their literal reality is mocked. The whole night's action is presented as a release of shaping fantasy which brings clarification about the tricks of strong imagination.

But Barber, too, found spiritual significance in the role the Fairies play in the comedy. He noted that in the 'epilogue' to the play (V.ii in the Everyman edition), Puck uses his broom both 'to sweep the dust behind the door' and to 'make "room" in the manner of the presenter of a holiday mummers' group. And with the dust, out go evil spirits.' What is more, Barber said,

The exorcism of evil powers complements the invocation of good. With their 'field dew consecrate', the fairies enact a lustration. Fertilizing and beneficent virtues are in festival custom persistently attributed to dew gathered on May mornings. Shakespeare's handling of nature has infused dew in this play with the vital spirit of moist and verdant woods. The dew is 'consecrate' in this sense. But the religious associations inevitably attaching to the word suggest also the sanctification of love by marriage. It is customary for the clergy, at least in important marriages, to bless the bed and bridal couple with holy water.

For Frank Kermode, writing on 'The Mature Comedies' in *Early Shakespeare* (Stratford-upon-Avon Studies 3, London, 1961), the Fairies were best viewed as agents of 'a "natural" force; a power that takes no account of civility or rational choice', and Puck in particular was 'a blinding Cupid'.

The juice used by Puck to bring confusion to the darkling lovers is possessed of all the force of Cupid's arrow, and is applied with equal randomness. The eye so touched will dote; in it will be engendered a fancy 'for the next live thing it sees'. Puck takes over the role of blind Cupid. The love he causes is a madness; the flower from which he gets his juice is called '*Love-in-idleness*', and that word has the force of wanton behaviour amounting almost to madness. . . . Puck attacks his task without moral considerations. . . .

R. W. Dent agreed with Kermode. In an article on 'Imagination in *A Midsummer Night's Dream*' (*Shakespeare Quarterly*, 1964), he observed that in this play

the origin of love never lies in reason. Love may be consistent with reason – e.g., Lysander is undeniably 'a worthy gentleman' – and a healthy imagination, although influenced by love, will not glaringly rebel against reason. But as Hermia initially indicates, her choice is dictated not by her judgment but by her 'eyes', by the vision of Lysander as her love-dictated imagination reports it.

As a consequence, Dent said,

The magic charm by which love is to be manipulated on this single night is quite naturally a flower potion administered on the eyes. From the play's beginning we are reminded of the commonplace that, although the eyes are integrally involved in the process of inspiring and transmitting love, nevertheless 'love sees not with the eyes';

instead, the eyes 'see' what the lover's imagination dictates. . . . Love, via imagination, transposes to 'form and dignity' by altering the normal evaluation, either in essence or in degree. At its extreme, it sees beauty where others see 'things base and vile', thus finding 'Helen's beauty in a brow of Egypt'.

Dent did not limit his remarks to the role imagination plays in the creation or complication of love relationships. He went on to discuss the Mechanicals' interlude, which he saw as 'a foil to the entire play of which it is a part, not merely to the portion involving the lovers'. And he commented at length on 'the principal member of Bottom's audience'.

Himself a creation from 'antique fable' unconsciously involved in 'fairy toys', Theseus believes in neither. . . . [His] estimation of such 'shadows' [as the players who present 'Pyramus and Thisbe'] is consistently deprecating. A noble governor, quite willing to accept poetry for a wedding-night pastime and to acknowledge it as the well-intended offering of his faithful subjects, he at no time implies any respect for it. Shakespeare's entire play implies a contrary view, despite the humility of its epilogue. . . .

In some measure, surely, *A Midsummer Night's Dream* is [a 'Defense of Dramatic Poesy'], although one that expesses its view by indirection and without the emphasis upon strictly moral edification one commonly finds in more formal defenses. . . . Theseus links lunatic, lover, and poet indiscriminately. Shakespeare, by contrasting the role of imagination in love with that in dramatic poetry, discriminates. As the play delightfully demonstrates, and lightly satirizes, the imagination in love often operates in defiance of 'discretion', especially in creating beauty observable by no one but the creator. Poetic art, distinct from that of a Quince or a Bottom, is in accord with discretion, and its creations are capable of universal appreciation, both as beautiful and as meaningful. . . . Rather than being a foe to good living, poetic imagination can be its comfort and its guide, far 'more yielding' than most dreams.

In 1964, in what turned out to be one of the most provocative books ever published on the playwright (*Shakespeare Our Contemporary*, London, 1964), Polish critic Jan Kott described *A Midsummer Night's Dream* as

the most erotic of Shakespeare's plays. In no other tragedy or comedy of his, except *Troilus and Cressida*, is the emotion expressed so brutally ... in this nightmarish summer night, the ass does not symbolise stupidity. Since antiquity and up to the Renaissance the ass was credited with the strongest sexual potency and among all quadrupeds is supposed to have the longest and hardest phallus. ...

The slender, tender and lyrical Titania longs for animal love. Puck and Oberon call the transformed Bottom a monster. The frail and sweet Titania drags the monster to bed, almost by force. This is the lover she wanted and dreamed of; only she never wanted to admit it, even to herself. Sleep frees her from inhibitions. The monstrous ass is being raped by the poetic Titania, while she still keeps on chattering about flowers.

[Eventually] Titania wakes up and sees a boor with an ass's head by her side. She slept with him that night. But now it is daylight. She does not remember ever having desired him. She remembers nothing. She does not want to remember anything.

Kott's book has struck some critics as wrongheaded, but one of its fruits was a 1970 Royal Shakespeare Company revival of *A Midsummer Night's Dream* by Peter Brook that is now regarded by many reviewers as the most compelling production the play – indeed, any Shakespearean play – has received in the last three and a half centuries. Robert Speaight described it vividly in his *Shakespeare Quarterly* theatre review for 1970. Noting that Peter Hall had staged the comedy twice at the Shakespeare Memorial Theatre at Stratford-upon-Avon (in 1959 and again in 1962), and had completed a film of it in 1968, Speaight said that

it seemed as if the only way you could give a new look to the *Dream* was to turn it into a nightmare. The paradoxical Professor Kott had already worked this transformation with his customary disregard of any evidence to the contrary; and since the admiration of Peter Brook and Professor Kott for one another was mutual and declared, I awaited Mr Brook's interpretation of the play with a curiosity not unmixed with apprehension.

It was eight years since Mr Brook had directed a play at Stratford, and one assumed that he would not have directed *Dream* unless he had something very particular to say about it. In fact, he forced one to forget – not, let me emphasize, the play itself – but anything one had seen done with it, or imagined being done with it, in the theater. He swept the mind of the spectator as clear as he had swept his stage, allowing the text of the play, beautifully and deliberately spoken, to play upon you with the freshness of words seen for the first time upon the printed page. He persuaded you to forget a century of theatrical tradition, with its conventions and clichés; and commanded you into a frame of mind where the very notion of magic, of supernatural agency, had to be created afresh.... The French have a phrase which communicates the peculiar, the explosively original, quality of this production. They speak of a *mystère en pleine lumière*, and this suggests the brilliant white light that Mr Brook threw upon his staring white stage, with only Titania's bright red feather bed to relieve it.

One saw nothing remotely resembling a tree – only coils of wire played out from a fishing rod over the iron railings which encircled the decor from above. One saw nothing resembling a fairy – but then we were not supposed to have been brought up on fairies.... There was much play with steel ladders and spinning tops ... [and] Oberon and Puck descended from the skies on swings with acrobatic agility. Indeed the virtuosities of the circus gave one a clue to Mr Brook's translation of midsummer magic into surrealism. Yes, one might object, but how can a play spun out of cobwebs and gossamer, and drenched in the morning dew, stand up to a treatment so metallic and so apparently defiant of mystery? The answer is that the mystery was all the deeper because it was seen so clearly – as clearly, no doubt, as it was once seen on the bare platform of the Globe. Because the words had no visual counterpart, they seized the imagination the more surely ... and there was never a moment's doubt after the opening performance that this one had taken its place in history.

Not everyone shared Robert Speaight's enthusiasm for the Peter Brook *Dream*. Writing in the *New Statesman* (4 September 1970), Benedict Nightingale described the production as 'perverse'.

The oddity of it is that Brook's controversial friend and influence, Professor Kott, is never more persuasive than when he condemns the sentimentality with which the *Dream* has been swaddled since Mendelssohn [wrote the score that dominated so many nineteenth-century productions of the play].... The effect of Brook's interpretation is to sentimentalise it once again, and in a new, more insidious way. His manic decoration has deprived it of suffering, fear, horror, and, apart from one moment, when Bottom's phallus is crudely mimed by the fairies, even of lust.

A later appraisal, by Sylvan Barnet in the revised Signet Classic text of *A Midsummer Night's Dream* (New York, 1986), includes the recollection that

The theatricality was ... emphasized by doubling: Theseus and Oberon were played by [the same performer]. ... No effort was made to disguise the doubling; the costumes were changed onstage. The point of this doubling (which has become a convention in almost all productions after Brook's) apparently was to suggest 1) that the action in the wood was a fantasy of Theseus's and Hippolyta's, or, to put it a little differently, beneath the civilized exteriors of Theseus and Hippolyta are the irrationalities of Oberon and Titania: and 2) that the play is very much a play, a theatrical entertainment and not a realistic imitation of the real world. ... Even the joke of using Mendelssohn's Wedding March while Bottom and Titania lolled in a hammock of ostrich feathers, as Puck and Oberon swung on trapezes, was good fun. At the end of the play, when the text calls for the fairies to bless the house, the entire cast left the stage, entered the aisles, and shook hands with members of the audience.

Among recent critical interpretations of *A Midsummer Night's Dream*, few have been as insightful as Anne Barton's introduction to the play in *The Riverside Shakespeare* (Boston, 1974). Among other things, she observes that

Theseus is a wise ruler and a good man, but Shakespeare makes it clear that there are other important areas of human experience with which he is incompetent to deal. When Theseus leads the bridal couples to bed at the end of Act V [Scene i] with the mocking reminder that "tis almost fairy time' he intends the remark as a last jibe at Hermia and Lysander, Helena and Demetrius: people who, in his estimation, have been led all too easily by darkness and their own fear to suppose a bush a bear. The joke, however, is on Theseus. It is indeed almost fairy time. In fact, Puck, Oberon and Titania have been waiting for this moment in order to take over the palace. For a few nocturnal hours the wood infiltrates the urban world. ... The life of the self-appointed critic of imagination and the irrational is permeated by exactly those qualities he is concerned to minimize or reject. Gently, the comedy suggests that while it is certainly possible to mistake a bush for a bear, one may also err as Theseus does by confounding a genuine bear with a bush. The second mistake is, on the whole, more dangerous.

In another publication of the same year, *The Words of Mercury: Shakespeare and English Mythography of the Renaissance* (Salzburg, 1974), Noel Purdon observes that in the Pyramus and Thisbe interlude Shakespeare

is parodying the play that he himself is writing. If we read the play-scene as his comment on his own efforts to provide a marriage-play, it has a double point.

The authors and producers of this play are as obsessed as he is with moonlight setting. They will rehearse by moonlight, they have set the action of their play by moonlight, they will perform it by moonlight, and they end up trying to represent Moonlight on the stage, a mistake in taste that Shakespeare is careful to avoid in his own play. . . . Quince . . . is preoccupied, as [contemporary playwright John] Lyly was, with the theatrical problem of bringing 'moonlight into a chamber'. Lyly, in one of his later plays, actually sets up on the stage a kind of giant astrolabe, in which the planets, including most importantly the Moon, move through a cycle of ascendancy and dominate the action on the stage before them. They exist as visible emblems which the spectators have to contemplate, hieratically enthroned in an upper gallery, and loaded with iconographical attributes . . . to make them readily identifiable. This is what Quince proposes to do – he will have an actor represent an icon. . . . Shakespeare indicates that he thinks this is liable to be poor dramatic practice – the notion illustrated will indeed be 'disfigured' rather than 'presented'. . . . Shakespeare himself prefers to use the poetry, not the actor, to represent the icon. . . .

Linda Bamber's *Comic Women, Tragic Men* (Stanford, 1982) describes *A Midsummer Night's Dream* as 'an anomaly among the festive comedies. It is unusual for the forces of the green world' of Shakespearean romantic comedy 'to be directed, as they are here, by a masculine figure', in this case Oberon, rather than, say, a Portia as in *The Merchant of Venice* or a Rosalind as in *As You Like It*.

Because the green world here is a partial reproduction of the social world, the feminine is reduced to a kind of first cause of the action while a masculine power directs it. In the other festive comedies the feminine Other presides. She does not *command* the forces of the alternative world, as Oberon does, but since she acts in harmony with these forces her will and desire often prevail.

Where are we to bestow our sympathies? On the forces [such as Hermia's refusal to obey her father] that make for the disruption of the status quo and therefore for the plot? or on the force [here Theseus] that asserts itself against the disruption and reestablishes a workable social order? Of course we cannot choose. We can only say that in comedy we owe our holiday to such forces as the tendency of the feminine to rebel, whereas to the successful reassertion of masculine power we owe our everyday order. Shakespearean comedy endorses both sides. Holiday is, of course, the subject and the analogue of each play; but the plays always end in a return to everyday life. The optimistic reading of Shakespearean comedy says that everyday life is clarified and enriched by our holiday from it, according to the pessimistic reading the temporary subversion of the social order has revealed how much that order excludes, how high a price we pay for it. But whether our return to everyday life is a comfortable one or not, the return itself is the inevitable conclusion to the journey out.

What to make of that 'return' will no doubt continue to be one of the questions that challenge interpreters, not only of *A Midsummer Night's Dream*, but of Shakespearean comedy in general.

FURTHER READING

Many of the works quoted in the preceding survey (or excerpts from them) can be found in modern collections of criticism. Of particular interest is a casebook, *Shakespeare: 'A Midsummer Night's Dream'*, edited by Antony Price (London: Macmillan, 1983), which includes selections from most of the authors cited above.

Other publications that include valuable discussions of the play:

Arthos, John, *Shakespeare's Use of Dream and Vision*, London: Bowes, 1977.

Berry, Ralph, *Shakespeare's Comedies: Explorations in Form*, Princeton: Princeton University Press, 1972.

Bonnard, Georges A., 'Shakespeare's Purpose in *A Midsummer Night's Dream*', *Shakespeare Jahrbuch*, 92 (1956).

Briggs, K. M., *The Anatomy of Puck*, London: Routledge & Kegan Paul, 1959.

Brown, John Russell, *Shakespeare and His Comedies*, London: Methuen, 1957.

Calderwood, James L., *Shakespearean Metadrama*, Minneapolis: University of Minnesota Press, 1971.

Cope, Jackson I., *The Theater and the Dream*, Baltimore: Johns Hopkins University Press, 1973.

Evans, Bertrand, *Shakespeare's Comedies*, London: Oxford University Press, 1960.

Fender, Stephen, *Shakespeare's 'A Midsummer Night's Dream'*, Studies in English Literature 35, London: Edward Arnold, 1968.

Garber, Marjorie, *Dream in Shakespeare*, New Haven: Yale University Press, 1974.

Hunter, G. K., *Shakespeare: The Late Comedies*, London: Longmans, Green, 1962.

Leggatt, Alexander, *Shakespeare's Comedy of Love*, London: Methuen, 1974.

Loney, Glenn, *Peter Brook's Production of William Shakespeare's 'A Midsummer Night's Dream' for the Royal Shakespeare Company*, Stratford-upon-Avon: RSC, 1974 (text as adapted for the production, plus comments by Brook and many of the actors).

Salingar, Leo, *Shakespeare and the Traditions of Comedy*, Cambridge: Cambridge University Press, 1974.

Warren, Roger, *'A Midsummer Night's Dream': Text and Performance*, London: Macmillan, 1983.

Young, David P., *Something of Great Constancy: The Art of 'A Midsummer Night's Dream'*, New Haven: Yale University Press, 1966.

Background studies and useful reference works:

Abbott, E. A., *A Shakespearian Grammar*, New York: Haskell House, 1972 (information on how Shakespeare's grammar differs from ours).

Allen, Michael J. B., and Kenneth Muir (eds), *Shakespeare's Plays in Quarto: A Facsimile Edition*, Berkeley: University of California Press, 1981.

Andrews, John F. (ed.), *William Shakespeare: His World, His Work, His Influence*, 3 vols, New York: Scribners, 1985 (articles on 60 topics).

Bentley, G. E., *The Profession of Player in Shakespeare's Time, 1590–1642*, Princeton: Princeton University Press, 1984.

Blake, Norman, *Shakespeare's Language: An Introduction*, New York: St Martin's Press, 1983 (general introduction to all aspects of the playwright's language).

Bullough, Geoffrey (ed.), *Narrative and Dramatic Sources of Shakespeare*, 8 vols, New York: Columbia University Press, 1957–75 (printed sources, with helpful summaries and comments by the editor).

Campbell, O. J., and Edward G. Quinn (eds), *The Reader's Encyclopedia of Shakespeare*, New York: Crowell, 1966.

Cook, Ann Jennalie, *The Privileged Playgoers of Shakespeare's London*: Princeton: Princeton University Press, 1981 (argues that theatre audiences at the Globe and other public playhouses were relatively well-to-do).

De Grazia, Margreta, *Shakespeare Verbatim: The Reproduction of Authenticity and the Apparatus of 1790*, Oxford: Clarendon Press, 1991 (interesting material on eighteenth-century editorial practices).

Eastman, Arthur M., *A Short History of Shakespearean Criticism*, New York: Random House, 1968.

Gurr, Andrew, *Playgoing in Shakespeare's London*, Cambridge: Cambridge University Press, 1987 (argument for changing tastes, and for a more diverse group of audiences than Cook suggests).

—— *The Shakespearean Stage, 1574–1642*, 2nd edn, Cambridge: Cambridge University Press, 1981 (theatres, companies, audiences, and repertories).

Hinman, Charlton (ed.), *The Norton Facsimile: The First Folio of Shakespeare's Plays*, New York: Norton, 1968.

Muir, Kenneth, *The Sources of Shakespeare's Plays*, New Haven: Yale University Press, 1978 (a concise account of how Shakespeare used his sources).

Onions, C. T., *A Shakespeare Glossary*, 2nd edn, London: Oxford University Press, 1953.

Partridge, Eric, *Shakespeare's Bawdy*, London: Routledge & Kegan Paul, 1955 (indispensable guide to Shakespeare's direct and indirect ways of referring to 'indecent' subjects).

Schoenbaum, S., *Shakespeare: The Globe and the World*, New York: Oxford University Press, 1979 (lively illustrated book on Shakespeare's world).

—— *Shakespeare's Lives*, 2nd edn, Oxford: Oxford University Press, 1992 (readable, informative survey of the many biographers of Shakespeare, including those believing that someone else wrote the works).

—— *William Shakespeare: A Compact Documentary Life*, New York: Oxford University Press, 1977 (presentation of all the biographical documents, with assessments of what they tell us about the playwright).

Spevack, Marvin, *The Harvard Concordance to Shakespeare*, Cambridge, Mass.: Harvard University Press, 1973.

Wright, George T., *Shakespeare's Metrical Art*, Berkeley: University of California Press, 1988.

PLOT SUMMARY

I.1   In his palace, Theseus, Duke of Athens, talks to Hippolyta, Queen
       of the Amazons, about their impending marriage. It is to be held in
       four days' time, when there will be a new moon. Egeus enters with
       his daughter, Hermia, and two young men, Lysander and Deme-
       trius. Egeus asks Theseus for his help. He wants his daughter to
       marry Demetrius, but she refuses, having fallen in love with
       Lysander. Theseus explains to Hermia that by Athenian law, if she
       refuses to comply with her father's wishes in this matter, she will
       either be put to death or must vow to become a nun. She must give
       Theseus her decision on his wedding day.
           Lysander refuses Demetrius' and Egeus' requests to give up
       Hermia's love, pointing out that Demetrius once courted Helena,
       who still loves him.
           Left alone, Lysander and Hermia plan to elope on the next night.
       They arrange to meet in the wood outside Athens, from where they
       will travel to the house of Lysander's aunt. There they can marry,
       safe from Athenian law.
           Helena, a friend of Hermia, enters, unhappy because of Deme-
       trius' love for Hermia. Hermia and Lysander comfort her by telling
       her their plan, and then they depart. Helena decides to tell
       Demetrius of the elopement, hoping this will endear her to him.

I.2   In Athens, a group of craftsmen meets to organise a production of
       the story of Pyramus and Thisby, which they hope to perform
       before Theseus and Hippolyta on their wedding night. The parts
       are given out and a secret rehearsal arranged for the following
       night in the wood outside Athens.

II.1   On the next night, in the wood, Puck, a sprite who serves Oberon,
       the King of the Fairies, meets a fairy who serves Titania, the Queen
       of the Fairies. He warns the fairy to keep Titania away from where
       they are, because Oberon, who is angry with Titania for her refusal
       to give him a changeling boy she has as her attendant, intends to
       spend the night here.

Oberon and Titania arrive at the same moment. Titania again refuses to give Oberon the changeling boy and then leaves. Oberon sends Puck to fetch a flower, intending to pour its juice onto Titania's eyes when she is asleep. This will make her fall in love with the first thing she sees upon waking. He will release her from this charm only when she has agreed to give him the changeling boy.

While Oberon stands by invisible, Demetrius enters, looking for Lysander and Hermia. Helena is following him, and he tries unsuccessfully to persuade her to leave him alone.

After they leave together, Puck returns with the flower. Oberon departs to pour the flower's juice onto Titania's eyes, having commanded Puck to do the same to the young Athenian man so that he will come to love the lady he was refusing.

II.2 Elsewhere in the woods, Titania is sung to sleep by her fairies. When they have left, Oberon enters, squeezes the flower's juice onto her eyes, and leaves. Lysander and Hermia appear, tired from their journey. They go to sleep a modest distance apart from one another. Puck arrives, and seeing the lovers' Athenian clothes presumes they are the couple about which Oberon talked. He pours the flower's juice onto Lysander's eyes and leaves.

Demetrius enters running, pursued by Helena. Having asked her to stop following him, Demetrius leaves and Helena, exhausted, remains. Seeing Lysander sleeping she wakes him, and he immediately falls in love with her. Helena does not believe his declarations of love and leaves. Lysander follows, leaving Hermia asleep and alone. Hermia awakes, and sets out to find Lysander.

III.1 At the Duke's Oak in the wood, the craftsmen meet to rehearse. They discuss problems of staging. As they begin to run through their lines, Puck comes in. When Bottom the weaver enters in the role of Pyramus, the rest of the cast run off terrified, because Puck has given Bottom the head of an ass. Puck sets off to chase the cast through the wood.

Bottom remains, unaware of his metamorphosis, and sings a song. This awakes Titania, who falls in love with him. With her fairies, she leads Bottom off to her bower.

III.2 Nearby, Oberon learns from Puck how Titania fell in love with Bottom. Then Hermia and Demetrius enter, he begging her to love him, and she begging him to tell her where her lover, Lysander, is. She leaves enraged, and he, despairing, lies down and goes to sleep.

Oberon realises that Puck has applied the flower's juice to the wrong young man. He sends Puck to find and bring Helena to him, and then pours juice from the flower into Demetrius's eyes.

Puck returns with Helena and Lysander, who is still trying to convince Helena of his love. Demetrius awakes, and falls in love with Helena. She does not believe his declarations, believing he and Lysander are mocking her. Hermia arrives, and Lysander tells her he now loves Helena. Helena believes that Hermia is party to the men's joke, Hermia that Helena has stolen Lysander from her; they quarrel. Lysander and Demetrius leave to fight for Helena's love. Helena runs away from the angry Hermia, who then herself departs.

Oberon sends Puck to ensure that Lysander and Demetrius do not meet, but instead wander through the wood until they fall asleep. Puck is then to pour the liquid from another herb into Lysander's eye. This herb removes the effects of the flower's juice. Meanwhile Oberon sets out to find Titania, to ask her again for the changeling boy and, if she grants his request, to undo the effects of the flower's juice upon her.

Puck carries out Oberon's orders. One at a time, he brings Lysander and Demetrius to the same spot, where they fall asleep. Afterwards Helena and then Hermia arrive and go to sleep. Puck applies the herb to Lysander's eyes.

IV.1 Nearby, watched by Oberon, Titania and her fairies entertain Bottom, who goes to sleep in Titania's arms. She dismisses the fairies, and then sleeps herself.

Puck arrives, and Oberon explains how he had met Titania earlier in the wood, and that she had given him the changeling boy. Oberon, applying the herb to Titania's eyes, wakes her, and then orders Puck to remove Bottom's ass's head. Amidst music Oberon, Titania and Puck leave.

Theseus and Hippolyta enter, with attendants. Having discovered the sleeping lovers, Theseus has them woken. As they explain how they came to be there, it emerges that all are now content, Lysander once more loving Hermia, and Demetrius now loving Helena. Overruling Egeus, Theseus invites the two couples to be married alongside himself and Hippolyta at the Temple. His party leaves for Athens and the two couples follow shortly after.

Bottom then awakes and, half-remembering what has happened to him, sets off home.

IV.2 In Athens, the other craftsmen are worrying over Bottom's absence, the marriage ceremonies having just finished. Bottom arrives with the news that they must go to Theseus's palace to present their play.

V.1   At the palace, Theseus and Hippolyta discuss what they have heard of the events of the previous night. The two couples enter, and Theseus, against the advice of Philostrate, his master of revels, decides that they will see the craftsmen's play.

The craftsmen come on and, after a prologue which explains their intents and the stage business to come, tell the tale of Pyramus and Thisby. Their audience conduct a running commentary. Finally two of the company dance, and then leave. It is past midnight, and Theseus dismisses everyone to their beds, declaring that they will celebrate every night for the next two weeks. Everyone departs.

V.2   Puck enters, soon followed by Oberon and Titania, with their attendant fairies. As the fairies sing and dance, Oberon orders everyone to wander through the palace until dawn, giving their blessings to the three couples. All but Puck leave to do so. He apologises in case any in the audience have not enjoyed themselves, and then departs.

ACKNOWLEDGEMENTS

Acknowledgements are due to the copyright holders of the extracts reprinted in the Perspectives on *A Midsummer Night's Dream* section of this edition.

DRAMA
IN EVERYMAN

The Oresteia
AESCHYLUS
*New translation of one of the
greatest Greek dramatic trilogies
which analyses the plays in
performance*
£5.99

Everyman and Medieval
Miracle Plays
edited by A. C. Cawley
*A selection of the most popular
medieval plays*
£4.99

Complete Plays and Poems
CHRISTOPHER MARLOWE
*The complete works of this great
Elizabethan in one volume*
£5.99

Restoration Plays
edited by Robert Lawrence
*Five comedies and two tragedies
representing the best of the
Restoration stage*
£7.99

Female Playwrights of the
Restoration: Five Comedies
edited by Paddy Lyons
*Rediscovered literary treasures
in a unique selection*
£5.99

Plays, Prose Writings
and Poems
OSCAR WILDE
*The full force of Wilde's wit
in one volume*
£4.99

A Dolls House/The Lady from
the Sea/The Wild Duck
HENRIK IBSEN
introduced by Fay Weldon
*A popular selection of Ibsen's
major plays*
£4.99

The Beggar's Opera and
Other Eighteenth-Century Plays
JOHN GAY et. al.
*Including Goldsmith's She Stoops
To Conquer and Sheridan's The
School for Scandal, this is a volume
which reflects the full scope of the
period's theatre*
£6.99

Female Playwrights of the
Nineteenth Century
edited by Adrienne Scullion
*The full range of female nineteenth-
century dramatic development*
£6.99

POETRY
IN EVERYMAN

**Amorous Rites: Elizabethan
Erotic Verse**
edited by Sandra Clark
*Erotic and often comic poems deal-
ing with myths of transformation
and erotic interaction between
humans and gods*
£4.99

Selected Poems
JOHN KEATS
*An excellent selection of the poetry
of one of the principal figures of
the Romantic movement*
£6.99

Poems and Prose
CHRISTINA ROSSETTI
*A new collection of her writings,
poetry and prose, marking the cen-
tenary of her death*
£5.99

Poems and Prose
P. B. SHELLEY
The essential Shelley in one volume
£5.99

**Silver Poets of the
Sixteenth Century**
edited by Douglas Brooks-Davies
*An exciting and comprehensive
collection*
£6.99

Complete English Poems
JOHN DONNE
*The father of metaphysical verse
in this highly-acclaimed collection*
£6.99

**Complete English Poems,
Of Education, Areopagitica**
JOHN MILTON
*An excellent introduction to
Milton's poetry and prose*
£6.99

Women Romantic Poets
1780 – 1830: **An Anthology**
edited by Jennifer Breen
*Hidden talent from the Romantic
era rediscovered*
£5.99

Selected Poems
D. H. LAWRENCE
*An authoritative selection
spanning the whole of Lawrence's
literary career*
£4.99

The Poems
W. B. YEATS
*Ireland's greatest lyric poet
surveyed in this ground-breaking
edition*
£7.99

All books are available from your local bookshop or direct from:
Littlehampton Book Services Cash Sales, 14 Eldon Way, Lineside Estate,
Littlehampton, West Sussex BN17 7HE (*prices are subject to change*)

To order any of the books, please enclose a cheque (in sterling) made payable to
Littlehampton Book Services, or phone your order through with credit card details (Access,
Visa or Mastercard) on 01903 721596 (24 hour answering service) stating card number
and expiry date. *(Please add £1.25 for package and postage to the total of your order.)*

In the USA, for further information and a complete catalogue call 1-800-526-2778